ANCIENT RUINS

OF THE SOUTHWEST

An Archaeological Guide

by David Grant Noble

Northland Publishing

for Ruth

FRONT COVER: Lomaki Ruin, photograph © 1991 by Scott Forehand
Cover design by David Jenney, © 1991 by Northland Publishing
Text design by Carolyn Gibbs

Composed and printed in the United States of America

FIRST REVISED EDITION, 1991
Second printing, 1993
Third printing, 1995
Fourth printing, 1996
ISBN 0-87358-530-5

Library of Congress Catalog Card Number 80-83016

The photographs, unless otherwise noted, are by the author.
All maps are current in 1993.

Excerpt from *The Professor's House*, by Willa Cather,
published by Alfred A. Knopf, Inc., New York, 1925.
Used with permission.

0651/7.5M/12-96

Contents

Preface

When the first edition of *Ancient Ruins of the Southwest* was released in 1981, I didn't think there would be a need to update it. But the field of archaeology, like other scientific disciplines, continues to move ahead, albeit at its own pace. As research methods evolve, new types of data spark fresh interpretations about how ancient people lived. Even modern people do not escape the scrutiny of archaeologists: Dr. William L. Rathje, a University of Arizona archaeologist, has gone so far as to analyze the trash Americans toss out daily as if it were archaeological data. Through this "garbage project," as his research has been dubbed, Dr. Rathje and his colleagues have achieved a unique view of our society's consumption habits.

Since *Ancient Ruins* was first published, much research has been completed on the intriguing and influential Anasazi culture associated with Chaco Canyon, and a plethora of new information has appeared on the Hohokam of the southern Arizona deserts. As this second edition goes to press, excavations continue at Sand Canyon and Lowry pueblos in Colorado and at Bandelier National Monument in New Mexico. In revising *Ancient Ruins*, I have incorporated the most up-to-date archaeological interpretations of southwestern cultural prehistory. Of course, researchers are not always in agreement about what happened and sometimes offer explanations that the next generation of researchers will disprove or modify.

I have selected more than a dozen newly opened sites for inclusion in this second edition. One of the most dramatic of these is Chimney Rock Pueblo in southern Colorado. Also new are Elden Pueblo and Casa Malpais in Arizona and Petroglyph

National Monument in New Mexico.

Another major development in southwestern archaeology in the past decade has been an increase in public interest. More and more people are going to see ruins, and each summer thousands of individuals—students, business people, retirees—participate as amateur researchers in public archaeological projects. Programs at Elden Pueblo and Sand Canyon are models in this trend. The growing interest in our native southwestern heritage is good for archaeology, for as more people learn about our cultural past, the more that past will be valued and safeguarded.

I wrote this book because I love to walk out into the canyons and deserts to look at and photograph ruins and rock art and contemplate their significance. I hope the words and photographs that follow inspire similar enjoyment on your part.

I would like to thank the following people for their assistance in developing the manuscript for this book: Kristie Arrington, Todd W. Bostwick, Doug Bowman, Bruce A. Bradley, J. J. Brody, R. B. Brown, Charles Cartwright, Jim Collerem, Larry Davis, John W. Hohmann, Winston Hurst, Doug Johnson, Anne Trinkle Jones, Richard W. Lang, Anthony Lutonski, Ruth J. Meria, Peter J. Pilles, Jr., Robert P. Powers, Cherie Scheick, Diane F. Souder, William B. Tsosie, Jr.

It goes almost without saying that a book such as this would never have been possible without the contributions of generations of archaeologists and without the efforts of many people and organizations who maintain and protect archaeological parks and preserves. My thanks to them also.

Introduction

No region of this continent and few areas of the world can boast a collection of archaeological ruins equal to that of the American Southwest. Due to unique geologic features and an arid climate, this vast expanse of mountains, deserts, and canyon-cut plateaus often has provided ideal environments for preserving even the most fragile artifacts.

It is to our considerable fortune that over the past 100 years, a few far-sighted individuals recognized the extraordinary cultural heritage of the Southwest and successfully campaigned to have certain archaeological treasures set aside as public monuments. These preserves constitute a far-flung and sometimes spectacular outdoor museum. They also represent but the gleaming tip of an iceberg under whose waterline lie archaeological sites numbering in the thousands. Blessed with such resources, it is possible for us today to see and understand the Southwest through its prehistory.

The area we know today as New Mexico, Arizona, southern Utah, and southern Colorado has sheltered and nurtured human beings for at least 12,000 years. Since the 1880s, archaeologists have displayed a consuming interest in trying to unravel the long complex history of these early people. The Folsom site in eastern New Mexico, where spear points were found embedded in the remains of a now-extinct species of bison, represents the first chapter of their long story. This story, as evidenced in Archaic campsites, Mogollon pithouses, Anasazi pueblos, and Spanish missions, has continued over thousands of years; there is no end in sight to human presence in the Southwest.

In an age such as our own, when the pace of external change

often exceeds our ability to adapt, ancient ruins can have more than a purely scenic or romantic appeal. Ruins are time anchors, giving substance to an elusive past. They are also the headstones, if you will, of deceased cultures. Ruins memorialize the successes and failures of our predecessors and remind us of the mortality of civilization.

Accustomed as most Americans are to physical comfort and convenience, it is natural to regard prehistoric Indian societies as having functioned at a very alien and primitive level. Technologically speaking, they did. And yet, putting aside contrasting material inventories, we soon discover that many elemental factors governing the development of ancient societies—climate, environment, and natural resources, for example—still remain of vital importance to our own well-being.

Were the Sinagua of the upper Little Colorado River any more awed by the 1064 eruption of Sunset Crater than we were by events at Mount St. Helens a few years ago? Was the Anasazis' search for firewood on the Mesa Verde any less urgent than our own quests for oil? How do *they* and *we* compare as victims of drought, flood, famine, disease, or warfare? Having an awareness of the continuing shared concerns of human beings over time and of repeated patterns of history only deepens and enlarges our appreciation of archaeological sites. With some understanding of prehistory, weatherworn petroglyphs and grassy pueblo mounds take on life. As for the towers of Hovenweep and cliff houses of Mesa Verde, they take on an aspect of discarded theatrical sets from an age-old drama whose cast has changed but whose theme may once again be replayed.

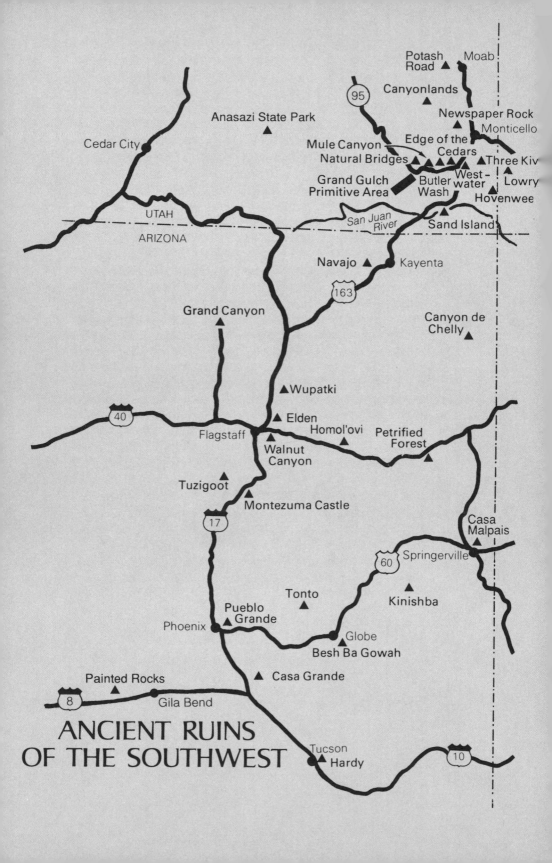

Potash Road

Moab

Canyonlands

(95)

Newspaper Rock

Monticello

Anasazi State Park

Mule Canyon
Natural Bridges

Edge of the
Cedars

Three Kiv

Cedar City

Grand Gulch
Primitive Area

Butler
Wash

West-
water

Lowry

Hovenwee

UTAH

San Juan
River

ARIZONA

Sand Island

Navajo

Kayenta

(163)

Canyon de
Chelly

Grand Canyon

Wupatki

(40)

Elden

Homol'ovi

Petrified
Forest

Flagstaff

Walnut
Canyon

Tuzigoot

Montezuma Castle

(17)

Casa
Malpais

(60)

Springerville

Tonto

Kinishba

Pueblo
Grande

Phoenix

Globe

Besh Ba Gowah

Painted Rocks

Casa Grande

(8)

Gila Bend

ANCIENT RUINS
OF THE SOUTHWEST

Tucson
Hardy

(10)

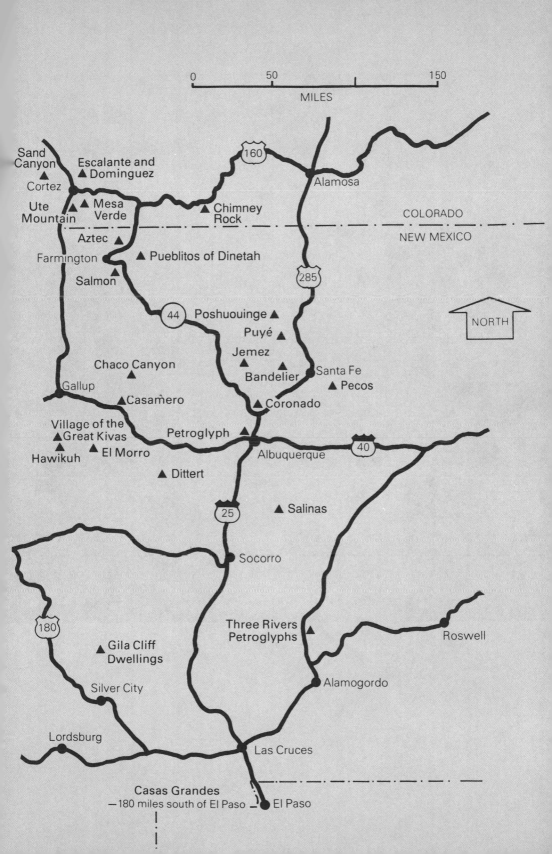

0 50 150
MILES

160

Sand
Canyon ▲
Cortez ▲
Ute ▲
Mountain

▲ Escalante and
  Dominguez

▲ Mesa
  Verde

▲ Chimney
  Rock

Alamosa

COLORADO
NEW MEXICO

Aztec ▲
Farmington
▲ Salmon

▲ Pueblitos of Dinetah

285

44 ▲ Poshuouinge ▲

▲ Puyé

Jemez ▲

Chaco Canyon
▲

Bandelier ▲

Santa Fe
▲ Pecos

NORTH

▲ Casamero

▲ Coronado

Gallup

Village of the
▲ Great Kivas
Hawikuh ▲   ▲ El Morro

Petroglyph ▲

Albuquerque

40

▲ Dittert

25

▲ Salinas

Socorro

180

Three Rivers
Petroglyphs ▲

Roswell

▲ Gila Cliff
  Dwellings

Silver City

Alamogordo

Lordsburg

Las Cruces

Casas Grandes
—180 miles south of El Paso ⚫ El Paso

Entrance of a reconstructed Mogollon pithouse.

THE MOGOLLON
Roots of Pueblo Culture

Pueblo culture in the Southwest had its roots among a people of shadowy origins who seemingly vanished long before Europeans arrived on American shores. These people are called the Mogollon (mug-ee-yone). They are important because they were the first people in the Southwest to cultivate corn, make pottery, and adopt a settled village life. These innovations were so successful that they spread throughout the Southwest and were key to the early evolution of Anasazi culture, which peaked in the eleventh through thirteenth centuries.

The Mogollon lived in small settlements in the wooded, well-watered highlands that curve down from the upper tributaries of the Little Colorado River, through the southern Arizona–New Mexico border country, to below Casas Grandes in Chihuahua, Mexico. This long mountainous arc lies to the south of the plateaus in which Anasazi culture later flourished and to the east of the desert river valleys that were the home of the Hohokam. Due perhaps to the diverse geography of their territory, the Mogollon were never a cohesive society; rather, they were a people whose dispersed hamlets shared basic cultural traits but also exhibited regional differences.

Mogollon culture evolved from an earlier Archaic period (5500 B.C. to A.D. 500) people—often referred to as the Cochise—who subsisted primarily as hunter-gatherers. Beginning about 1000 B.C., the Cochise began a long slow process in which they depended less on their seasonal rounds of foraging and more upon horticulture. The main catalyst for this change was the introduction of corn (maize) from Mexico, where it had been under cultivation for 5,000 years or more. Corn itself had evolved

Sketch of Mogollon pithouse.

from wild teosinte in the southern Mexican highlands. During its evolution from a wild grass to a domestic crop, seed size was increased at the expense of seed dispersal by wind, and it grew dependent upon human cultivation for survival. Archaeologists theorize that the Mogollon were drawn to corn cultivation (and later bean, squash, and bottle gourd) because the harvests were more dependable and predictable than that of wild plants. As seasons passed, the Mogollon developed plant strains that were better adapted to their environment, and they learned how to attain greater yields through improved agricultural methods. Farming meant staying near cultivated fields to protect plants from animals and working cooperatively, and that, in turn, led to the formation of villages. Living in pithouses grouped in hamlets necessitated new social interactions different from those of their nomadic life.

Early, small villages were usually situated on high ground. Later, probably for convenience, the people moved their homes closer to their cultivated fields in the valleys. The typical pithouse was a small round or oblong structure built over a shallow excavation with low slab-lined walls and a hard dirt floor in which cysts were dug for storage. Interior upright posts supported roof timbers that were often raised in a conical formation and overlaid with sticks, grass, and a layer of dirt. The house was entered through a tunnel-like door at one side. Villages often had fifteen or twenty pithouses, one of which usually was larger so that it could be used for religious and community functions.

Pottery was developed among the Mogollon and was a definite improvement over basketry for carrying water, cooking, and the safe storage of seeds. To the archaeologist, ceramics are of inestimable value, for they are nonperishable and help date the sites in which they are found and identify the culture of their makers.

From about A.D. 1000 to 1250, a branch of the Mogollon culture known as the Mimbres thrived in southwest New Mexico. The Mimbres produced decorated pottery in which people, birds, animals, fish, mythic figures, and abstract designs were exquisitely drawn in paint. This unique ceramic decoration offers fascinating insights into the daily and spiritual life of the Mimbres. So sought after are Mimbres bowls that an illicit trade has developed, resulting in the wholesale destruction of many sites in the Mimbres region.

After A.D. 1000, Mogollon culture began to be influenced by the stronger and more expansive Anasazi, who lived on the Colorado Plateau to the north. This influence is most apparent at Gila Cliffs in Mogollon territory, where, for example, the architecture resembles that of Mesa Verde cliff dwellings. But the Mogollon were also influenced from the south, especially from the large population and trading center at Casas Grandes. In fact, after the early introduction of innovations, Mogollon culture evolved little and became susceptible to the cultural influences of its more dynamic neighbors. By A.D. 1450, they had completely abandoned their highlands and had merged physically and culturally with the Anasazi.

Readers may wonder why the Mogollon are represented in the present guide by only a handful of sites. This is largely because they built dwellings with perishable materials that returned to nature after being abandoned. Gila Cliff Dwellings is an exception to the rule. To reconstruct a pithouse hamlet would be an interesting and by no means impossible task, but public support for such a project has not yet materialized and seems improbable in the near future. It seems that pithouses do not beguile the imagination as do Anasazi cliff dwellings. Still, as we enjoy the spectacular ruins of the Anasazi, we should not forget how important the introduction of corn, pottery, and settled village life were to the evolution of human culture in the Southwest.

Suggested reading: *Mogollon Culture Prior to A.D. 1000*, by Joe Ben Wheat, American Anthropological Association Memoir 82, 1955.

Mimbres bowl. School of American Research Collections.

Gila Cliff Dwellings National Monument

Gila Cliff Dwellings National Monument is at the end of New Mexico 15, 44 miles (2 hours driving time) north of Silver City, in southwestern New Mexico.

Gila Cliff Dwellings resemble more the villages of Mesa Verde Anasazi far to the north than those of the Mogollon, who, through most of their history, lived in humble semisubterranean pithouses. The appearance of Puebloan-style cliff houses in the midst of Mogollon country illustrates the geographically broad influence of the Anasazi in the thirteenth century.

The earliest archaeological site found within the national monument is, in fact, a Mogollon-style pithouse, built in the open some 1,000 years before the cliff dwellings. The Mogollon continued to live in this area through the centuries, but after about A.D. 1000, they became more and more influenced by the Anasazi. This influence is most apparent in house style but is evident in other elements of material culture as well.

At Gila Cliffs, visitors can see forty masonry rooms built in the shelter of five deeply recessed caves that are elevated 150 feet or more above the canyon floor. Despite early looting and vandalism at the site, the pueblo's walls are remarkably well preserved. Dates obtained from original roof timbers show that the Mogollon built these dwellings in the 1270s or 1280s and probably abandoned them within a couple of generations.

The ten or fifteen families who lived here raised crops on the mesas and cultivated garden plots along portions of the streambeds. Like all prehistoric southwestern Indians, they also subsisted by collecting a variety of native plants and seeds, hunting game, and trading with neighboring communities for other supplies and commodities they needed.

Visitors to Gila Cliffs should first pick up a trail guide at the visitor center, then proceed to the trailhead, which is just over a mile away. The mile-long trail crosses the West Fork of the Gila River, winds up Cliff Dwellers Canyon about half a mile, then loops back to the caves. In the shade of tall pines, this scenic walk initially follows the creek, then leads into some steeper climbing. You are able to enter all but one of the caves and walk among the cliff dwellings, which offer fine picture-taking opportunities. From the ruins, the trail returns by a different route to the river and parking area. You should plan at least half an hour for the tour and longer for a more leisurely sightseeing walk.

Ruins at Gila Cliff Dwellings.

Gila Cliff Dwellings National Monument encompasses only 533 acres but is surrounded by over three million acres of national forest, one of the most beautiful and primitive regions of North America. The monument, in fact, is jointly operated by the U.S. Forest Service and the National Park Service.

In the late 1800s, this country was a stronghold of the Chiricahua Apaches, some of whose leaders—Mangas Colorado, Cochise, Victorio, and Geronimo—have become legendary figures of Indian resistance to European-American expansion in the Southwest. Today, the Gila Wilderness, with over 2,000 miles of trails, is a paradise for hikers, backpackers, and packtrippers. You can roam this area for weeks and only meet a few other souls.

A forest service campground is maintained near the monument, and gas, food, camping supplies, lodging, horse rentals, and guided pack trips are available at nearby Gila Hot Springs.

Three Rivers Petroglyph Site

Three Rivers is an intersection along U.S. 54, 30 miles north of Alamogordo, New Mexico. To reach the petroglyph preserve, turn east at this intersection and proceed for 5 miles to the entrance to the site's parking lot. From here, one trail leads through the petroglyph area and another to excavated ruins.

Rock art is found throughout areas of the Southwest where Native American people lived, traveled, hunted, drew water, or performed religious ceremonies. The images have often survived in remarkably fine condition over many centuries. Rock art sites are widely scattered, often located on privately owned land, in remote canyons, or in places where protection from vandalism has not been feasible. Many sites, while well known to archaeologists and local residents, are rarely seen and appreciated by the general public. Except in reproduction, petroglyphs and pictographs cannot be exhibited in museums, and in the past, most archaeologists have failed to regard rock art as a serious subject of research. In recent years, however, thoughtful studies have been conducted on rock art, and some researchers have consulted Native Americans concerning their interpretations of the images. One such study is Jane Young's fine book, *Signs from the Ancestors* (University of New Mexico Press, Albuquerque, New Mexico, 1988).

A petroglyph (from the Greek *petros*, "stone," and *glyphe*, "carving") is an image that has been pecked, chiseled, grooved, or scratched on a rock surface. Petroglyphs were usually made by rubbing or striking with a stone against a darkened rock surface, such as the face of a cliff or boulder. Sometimes, to achieve greater control,

Petroglyph of mountain sheep at Three Rivers.

a chisel stone was placed against the rock and then struck with a heavier hammer stone. The end result was to chip off the darker oxidized exterior, or patina, exposing a lighter undersurface. Petroglyphs vary greatly, from thinly scratched, seemingly thoughtless scrawls, to more deeply etched stylized representations of the natural or supernatural world, to carefully conceived designs and narrative pictures.

The Three Rivers Petroglyph Site is one of only a few places in the Southwest that have been set aside solely for their rock art. Some 20,000 glyphs representing humans, animals, birds, fish, reptiles, insects, and plants, as well as various geometric and abstract designs, are scattered over fifty acres of a long ridge near the western base of the Sacramento Mountains, in the south-central portion of New Mexico.

The Three Rivers petroglyphs were created by Jornada Mogollon people between ca. A.D. 900 and 1400. A Mogollon village site lies a couple hundred yards south of the petroglyph ridge, and its inhabitants were probably responsible for the inscriptions. This site has been partially excavated and lies along an interpretive trail. What motivated the glyph-making, however, is not known.

The petroglyphs appear grayish white on the dark surface of

boulders. Many seem crude, sketchy, and hard to comprehend or translate into familiar life forms. But others clearly were executed by accomplished artists. Viewers familiar with Mimbres pottery will recognize a similarity between some of these images and those that appear on Mimbres ceramics. A trail nearly a mile long winds along the ridge passing many of the more interesting images; thousands more, however, can be found by digressing from the path.

Although the Three Rivers site is often uncomfortably hot, or cold and windy, and you have to invest time to see much of the rock art, an excursion here is well worth the time and effort. There is also a fine view over the surrounding Tularosa Basin. You can sit among the boulders to contemplate the spirit images of a long-ago people or reflect on the little-known events this scenic desert landscape must have witnessed. Were the petroglyph artists doodling, expressing thoughts and concepts, recording events, communicating to their gods, practicing magic? And what became of the people? Scholars have few answers to such questions. Another disturbingly poignant aspect of this area's past occurred in relatively recent years. In the early morning hours of 16 July 1945, an observer at this site would have witnessed the awesome explosion of the world's first atomic bomb.

At the parking lot, visitors will find picnic tables, barbecue pits, drinking water, and toilets; overnight camping is permitted. Also, a National Forest Service campground is located several miles away, and motels can be found in Alamogordo and Carrizozo. Other nearby places of interest include the Mescalero Apache reservation east of Tularosa, White Sands National Monument, and the historic town of Lincoln.

> Suggested reading: *Archaeological Survey, Three Rivers Drainage, New Mexico,* by Mark Wimberly and Alan Rogers, El Paso Archaeological Society, El Paso, Texas, 1977.

Casas Grandes

The Casas Grandes ruins are located just outside the village of Casas Grandes, Chihuahua, Mexico, approximately 180 miles southwest of Ciudad Juarez, Chihuahua, and El Paso, Texas, along Mexico 2.

Perhaps the most impressive prehistoric ruin in the Southwest is the Casas Grandes site in Mexico. In size alone, Casas Grandes, which is twenty-seven times larger than Chaco Canyon's Pueblo Bonito, is in a category of its own; the levels of technological and commercial sophistication achieved by its inhabitants were unsur-

Ruins of Paquimé at Casas Grandes.

passed by any indigenous community in the American Southwest.

Casas Grandes is located in the Chihuahua Desert of northern Mexico in a broad valley that receives ten to twenty inches of rain annually plus the drainage from 18,000 square miles of surrounding mountains. The basin and range topography of this region extends unbroken into southern New Mexico and Arizona, and the Casas Grandes people maintained active cultural and economic links with groups from these more northern areas. The varied environment of the Casas Grandes region, ranging from desert flats to high mountains, was fully utilized by its inhabitants who increased in numbers and developed a thriving trade center.

A significant portion of Paquimé, Casas Grandes's core city, was excavated by the Amerind Foundation of Dragoon, Arizona, between 1958 and 1961. The results of this major research project have since been published in a series of illustrated volumes, including more than a thousand pages of synthesis by its director, the late Charles C. Di Peso (see suggested readings).

Sometime after A.D. 1000, the people of Paquimé began to construct multistoried rammed-earth buildings. Two centuries later, some archaeologists argue, they became profoundly influenced by an influx of *puchtecas* from the south. These entrepreneurs, who represented Mesoamerican trading guilds far to the south, recognized the potential of Casas Grandes as a commerical base and moved up to organize local support. Under their leadership, Paquimé became the nucleus of an empire with thousands of satellite or culturally associated villages. It had dominion over a vast area of what is now northwestern Chihuahua and northeastern Sonora and control over a trading network reaching hundreds of miles to the north.

Di Peso likens the Casas Grandes system of commerce to that of the Hudson Bay Company in Canada, whose cadre of traders and network of trading posts brought materials and ideas across vast distances between culturally disparate societies. In the Casas Grandes case, prime trade items included parrots, parrot feathers, copper bells, sea shells, and such semiprecious stones as turquoise rather than pelts.

The commercial success of Casas Grandes fed directly into the city itself as evidenced in its remarkable growth that resulted in an extensive urban renewal sometime after the mid-1200s. Large marketplaces were built as well as warehousing facilities, ceremonial mounds, plazas, ball courts, and a complex of high-rise apartment buildings. Di Peso speculated that the dramatic architecture of Paquimé probably was planned in part to entice large numbers of visitors from the hinterlands to further "fill the larders of the city and its masters." No doubt such a strategy was successful, and as power focused on the city, its leaders were probably able to recruit rural folk for the construction of the extraordinary water control system.

This system began to the northwest of the city at Ojo Vareleño (Vareleño Springs), which today produces over 3,000 gallons of water per minute. This flow was brought to Paquimé in aquaducts and stored in a reservoir from which it was dispensed in underground stone-lined channels that serviced the main house clusters. Drainage tunnels and large subterranean walk-in cisterns were other features of the system.

In addition to a domestic water system, Casas Grandes inhabitants enjoyed the benefits of heated sleeping platforms, airy living-room spaces, raised-platform cooking hearths, city parks, and what must have been a vibrant marketplace complex. Some of the plazas were bordered by rows of turkey and macaw pens; aviculture is believed to have been a principal source of wealth and renown.

Sometime after A.D. 1400, the sociopolitical system of Casas Grandes began to come apart, and the city fell into increasing disrepair. Civil construction and public maintenance ceased, and the society suffered from a crippling economic depression. The causes of Paquimé's collapse are not known, but we can reasonably speculate that if commerce brought about the city's rise, a trading slump was responsible for its fall. Other scenarios, however, such as a climatic shift, disease, or a regional revolt, may possibly have been causal factors. Whatever the circumstances, when Europeans first entered the area more than a century later, they found the ancient city in ruins and the valley abandoned.

Thanks to an arid climate, the massiveness of the buildings, and stabilization work by the Mexican government, the Casas Grandes site has not experienced heavy erosional damage since the archaeological excavations were completed. Floor features, of course, have disappeared, and the temple mounds are gullied, but the high adobe walls of former buildings still stand, and when visiting the ruins, you quickly become aware that a powerful and superbly organized society once existed here. In this sense, interesting comparisons can be made to the complex at Chaco Canyon (see p. 119) in northern New Mexico and to Hohokam towns such as Casa Grande (see p. 22) in southern Arizona.

As of 1991, minimal education is offered at the Casas Grandes site but interpretive signs along the ruins trail are planned. The volumes by Di Peso make excellent background reading for people interested in Paquimé's past. In addition, educational groups seeking a knowledgeable guide may contact Julian Hernandez or R. B. Brown, c/o Preparatoria Federal por Cooperacion, Ave. Colon No. 1201, Col. Industrial, Nuevo Casas Grandes, 31700 Chihuahua, Mexico [telephone (169) 4-2220].

While traveling to or from the ruins, many people will be interested in taking a stroll around the historic plaza of the nearby town of Casas Grandes. Here you can gain a sense of local Mexican life and culture and, perhaps, even catch the ambiance of Hispanic villages in New Mexico a century ago. The city of Nuevo Casas Grandes, which is several kilometers from the ruins, has motels, restaurants, gas stations, and other travel services. The highways to Columbus, New Mexico, and El Paso, Texas, are well marked and in good condition.

Suggested reading: *Casas Grandes: A Fallen Trading Post of the Gran Chichimeca*, 3 vols., by Charles C. Di Peso, Northland Press, Flagstaff, Arizona, 1974.

Casa Malpais

Casa Malpais is located less than a mile west of Springerville, Arizona, off U.S. 60. To visit the site, contact the Casa Malpais Visitor Center at 318 West Main Street in Springerville or call (602) 333-5375 for information. These ruins are presently being developed as an archaeological park, which is scheduled to formally open in 1992.

Casa Malpais is one of the more unusual ruins described in this book. Like Gila Cliff Dwellings (see p. 5), it was inhabited by Mogollon people between about A.D. 1250 and 1400, but this site bears little resemblance to any other ruins in the Southwest. Its principal features include a masonry pueblo of more than fifty rooms, a great kiva, several small residential compounds, and a massive stone wall that surrounds the main group of ruins. In addition, there are segments of prehistoric trails, two masonry stairways that mount the basalt cliff behind the site, rock art panels, and a rare complex of subterranean ceremonial chambers.

Casa Malpais ("badlands house") is true to its name because the village was built against the eroded edge of an ancient lava flow and was constructed of its basaltic rocks. The fracturing and slumping of the lava cliffs tens of thousands of years ago created a series of narrow terraces upon which some Mogollon people situated their village. Just below the site to the south flows the Little Colorado River, a relatively constant source of water. The riparian habitat that once flourished around the river no doubt provided a wide variety of game and plant foods to local people. Additionally, seasonal river flooding created rich alluvial soils to support agriculture. Farming would have further benefited from the region's thirty-inch average rainfall, double that of many parts of the American Southwest.

A unique aspect of Casa Malpais is its inspiring surrounding landscape. A vast lava-flow plain extends to the north of the site. To the south and east lies Round Valley, a scenic basin with a 7,000-foot elevation, used historically by sheepherders and horse thieves. A large volcanic field, marked by rounded cinder cones and lava-capped mesas, extends to the north and west.

This region may have seen a scattering of small Mogollon pithouse villages as early as A.D. 700. Certainly, between A.D. 900 and 1100, the area's population was on the increase, and by the end of this period, pueblo-style architecture was becoming more apparent in the area's Mogollon communities.

Apart from past archaeological surveys and minor testing (and pothunting), Casa Malpais is a "virgin" site. The main pueblo has the appearance of a rubbled mound, although some room outlines are distinguishable. The most impressive single ruin is

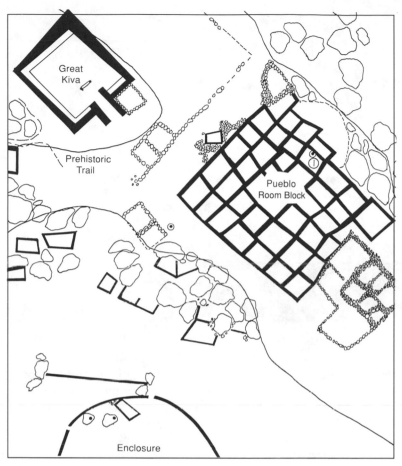

Plan of a portion of the Casa Malpais site.
Courtesy Louis Berger & Associates, Inc.

the square great kiva whose massive rock walls still stand between four and eight feet in height. An unusual feature are the catacombs, which lie in deep fissures in the lava around the site, that once contained an estimated 200 burials. However, since most of this material was looted over the years and the crevaces are dangerous, there is no public access. To reach the top of the lava mesa north of the site, the Casa Malpais villagers modified two natural clefts in the cliff behind their settlement by arranging boulders to form rough stairways. Visitors can easily climb these today and are rewarded by a view from the top over miles of landscape.

With an apparent good water supply, rich farming soils, and a varied environment for hunting and gathering, why did the Mogollon disappear from Casa Malpais and the region? The causes of population shifts over time in the Southwest are continually debated, but experts generally agree that climate change, especially

Casa Malpais along the lava escarpment.

drought, had an impact on the natural environment and the ability of people to survive. Fluctuating amounts of moisture probably accounted for both the Mogollon settling and eventually abandoning Casa Malpais.

Apaches, a nonagricultural nomadic people, are believed to have migrated into this region beginning in the late 1600s, and European-American herders and settlers began moving here some 200 years later. As the town of Springerville developed, the ruins of Casa Malpais began increasingly to suffer from vandalism and pothunting. Curiosity about the ruins led to explorations into the catacombs to collect grave goods and dig into the pueblo in search of pots. Even so, the site as a whole remains remarkably intact both for potential future research and for enjoyment as a cultural park. A visit here, expecially after interpretive trails have been established, should be included on any ruins tour.

Springerville has restaurants, gas stations, and lodging. Other archaeological sites in the region are Homol'ovi Ruins State Park (see p. 101) and Petrified Forest National Park (see p. 104).

Suggested reading: "Casa Malpais, A Fortified Pueblo Site at Springerville, Arizona," by Edward B. Danson and Harold E. Molde, *Plateau* 22 (4), 1950.

THE HOHOKAM
Ancient Dwellers of the Desert

The Hohokam were one of the Southwest's seminal cultures. Centered in the Phoenix Basin of south-central Arizona, their influence, especially through trading, reached west to the California coast, east into the Great Plains, south into Mesoamerica, and north to the Rocky Mountains. Today, the Hohokam are most remembered for several remarkable achievements: some 500 miles of canals; ball courts and platform mounds; and finely made craft arts, such as jewelry, pottery, and mosaics.

Most working archaeologists today believe that the Hohokam emerged in southern Arizona out of a long, preexisting tradition of Archaic hunters and gatherers. But another school of thought holds that the Hohokam initially migrated north into southern Arizona from lands lying today in Mexico. Whichever hypothesis eventually proves the more accurate, the Hohokam had formed a distinct culture by around A.D. 1, when its members were emphasizing agriculture over foraging and producing polished redware pottery. During the succeeding fourteen centuries, the Hohokam developed an increasingly complex culture, which reached its fullest expression after A.D. 1100 but by 1400 had slipped into decline. By A.D. 1450, Hohokam culture no longer existed or had changed to such an extent that it could no longer be recognized in the archaeological record.

One of the most prominent features of Hohokam culture is a vast network of hand-dug irrigation canals. The main canals, some of which are seventy-five feet across the top and fifty feet wide at the bottom, fed thousands of smaller ditches that brought water to an estimated 25,000 acres of cultivated fields. The Hohokam established villages at regular intervals along the main canals to

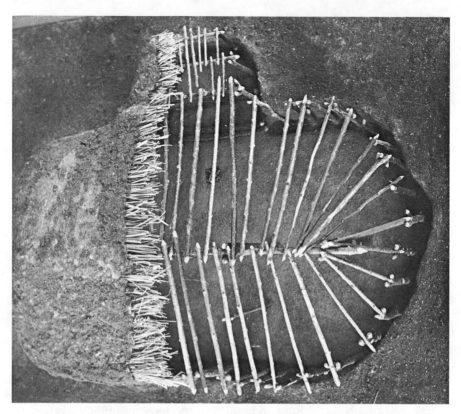

Cut-away model of Hohokam house.

create a complex, interlocking social and economic system that more than anything else explains the remarkable success of their long-lasting society. Through their organizational and engineering skills, combined with a deep pool of human labor, they literally transformed portions of the Sonoran Desert into a garden to serve their needs.

Hohokam villages, for the most part, were less remarkable architecturally than those of their Anasazi neighbors to the north. Apparently built without concern for defense, the houses were randomly spread over a large area. The common folk lived in simple dwellings built of sticks and mud that eventually melted into the desert leaving little trace. The concentrated and compact pueblo-style of the Anasazi held little appeal to these Sonoran Desert dwellers.

But the Hohokam did build some large-scale public structures, such as ball courts, over 200 of which have been found in Arizona. Oval in form, they ranged from seventy-five feet long and forty-five feet wide to nearly triple that size. Within the excavated playing field, it is thought, a ritual contest was played that had

Ball court at Wupatki.

its origins in Mesoamerica. This game, as witnessed by early Spaniards in Mexico, involved knocking a hard rubber ball up and down the court, using only hips or arms. As interpreted by anthropologist David R. Wilcox, the game was a microcosm of the universe that "simulated the movements of the deities in an effort to make the world a liveable place for humans."

Large earthen platform mounds at the center of villages represent another form of Hohokam monumental architecture, especially after A.D. 1100. The mounds were surrounded by clusters of houses within adobe compound walls. Fifty sites contain these platform mounds, some of which have as much as 32,000 cubic yards of fill and are topped by small temple ruins. A good example can be seen at Pueblo Grande (see p. 19) in Phoenix, Arizona. Rituals and dances to please the gods probably were held on the mounds at certain times of the year. Around A.D. 1300, residences began to be built on top of the mounds, suggesting the appearance of an elite or ruling class of people.

The Hohokam were highly skilled craftspeople. Typically, pottery is most abundant in the archaeological record, including red-on-buff vessels and clay figurines. The Hohokam fashioned pallets, bowls, and a variety of tools and weapons out of stone. They also excelled in the production of shell ornaments, such as beads, rings, bracelets, and pendants. They often etched designs

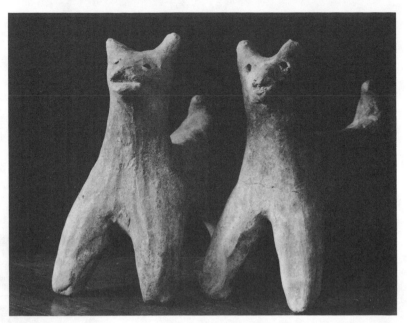

Hohokam animal figurines from Pueblo Grande.
Courtesy Soil Systems, Inc., and Phoenix Arts Commission.

into the shells using an acid solution made from fermented saguaro juice. This was a uniquely Hohokam art form.

We are inclined to praise cultures for the material objects they left behind: in the case of the Hohokam—canals, ball courts, mounds, and crafts. But we only have to drive across the desert in the summer months to realize the most remarkable achievement of these people—survival in an extraordinarily challenging environment. Their unsurpassed knowledge of their natural world and innovative approach to dealing with it allowed them to prosper for 1,500 years. They harnessed the region's precious water resources; harvested more than 200 species of wild plants with nutritious seeds and fruits; hunted birds and mammals; and cultivated extensive fields of corn, beans, squash, cotton, and agave.

It is widely assumed that the Pima and Tohono O'Odham (Papago) people of historic and modern times are the descendents of the Hohokam. This assumption is based on native oral traditions as well as clues in the archaeological and historical records. Hohokam culture evidently came to an end around A.D. 1450, although the population of the region had fallen into decline before then. But the people, though reduced in numbers, lived on, adapting in different ways to new challenges. Over the course of succeeding generations, they held onto some traditions, abandoned others, and developed a complex of new customs and practices. In this respect, their story follows a universal pattern.

Visitors to southern Arizona will enjoy seeing Pueblo Grande (below) in Phoenix, Casa Grande (see p. 22) near Coolidge, and Painted Rocks (see p. 26) west of Gila Bend. In addition, the Hardy Site (p. 28) in Tucson's Fort Lowell Park is a small tribute to this culture. Beyond seeing these sites, you should visit the Arizona State Museum in Tucson and the cultural centers on various Indian reservations.

> Suggested reading: *The Hohokam: Desert Farmers and Craftsmen*, by Emil W. Haury, The University of Arizona Press, Tucson, Arizona, 1976.

Pueblo Grande Ruins

Pueblo Grande Ruins and Museum are located on the southeast corner of Washington and 44th streets on the east side of Phoenix, Arizona. From Interstate 10, take the Hohokam Expressway or 48th Street exit northbound.

The Salt River rises in the White Mountains of east-central Arizona, flows through Roosevelt Reservoir in the Tonto Basin, and descends to the broad agricultural flatlands around Phoenix. Along the north bank of the Salt lies the partially excavated prehistoric village site of Pueblo Grande, first occupied more than 1,400 years ago. Pueblo Grande was one of the largest of some twenty Hohokam communities spaced at approximately three-mile intervals along the extensive agricultural canals developed by these desert farmers.

At its peak in the late Classic period (ca. A.D. 1300), Pueblo Grande probably covered a two-square-mile area, mostly to the north and east of the present-day Pueblo Grande Museum. Today, portions of this town lie hidden beneath the buildings and streets of Phoenix. But in its heyday, it would have presented an impressive sight, since it included uncounted residential compounds, a "big house" similar to that of Casa Grande, a twenty-foot-high platform mound as big as a football field covered with houses, at least two ball courts, and a sea of small peasant dwellings. It is thought that more than a thousand people inhabited the village.

In the last century, when the rich agricultural potential of the Phoenix Basin was rediscovered by European-American settlers, the Pueblo Grande site was put under cultivation to produce cotton. Even the three-story big house was demolished and its fill was used to help level fields. The platform mound, however, was preserved because it contained too much stone to make leveling feasible. It is this feature and the adjacent ball court and muse-

View from the Pueblo Grande platform mound.

um that constitute the site's present-day focus. The mound, with approximately 32,000 cubic yards of fill (comparable to more than 100,000 wheelbarrow loads), dominated its environs. It appears to have been built in phases over a number of generations. Researchers have estimated that, in theory, one hundred people working one month a year could have completed the job in twenty-four years. In fact, the mound was built in phases over a 200-year period.

The mound was retained by a massive wall consisting of hardened chunks of caliche and river rocks. Houses and other specialized structures stood both on and around it to form a residential and ceremonial compound that was contained by another perimeter wall. Who lived in this special area within the larger Pueblo Grande town? Possibly an elite or priestly class of people who derived their power from control of the canals and success as traders and merchants. From the tops of the mounds they would have enjoyed a physical position reflecting their status in the entire community and would have been able to survey the town, fields, canals, valley, and distant mountain ranges. Today, of course, the view is dominated by a freeway, international airport, and urban sprawl.

Nowhere in the Southwest is there a more stark contrast between pre-Columbian and modern America than at Pueblo Grande. Rush-hour traffic speeds by a thirteenth-century ball court and jumbo passenger jets touch down just beyond a thousand-year-old canal.

Archaeologists have investigated Pueblo Grande sporadically since Adolph F. Bandelier's brief visit there in 1883. The first professional excavation at the site was conducted four years later by the Mary Hemenway Southwestern Archaeological Expedition, whose main focus of research, however, was another site across the river, Pueblo de los Muertos. Unfortunately, over the years little research has been published about Pueblo Grande; consequently contemporary scholars have given the site scant attention. But two recent developments promise to change Pueblo Grande's low profile among archaeologists. First, between 1988 and 1990, archaeologists from Soil Systems, Inc., excavated a large portion of the village ruins situated in the path of the then-planned Hohokam Expressway to the north and east of the museum. Here they uncovered abundant village remains from the Classic period (A.D. 1100–1450) and earlier, including numerous cemeteries. Reports on these findings will begin appearing in 1991. Second, the Pueblo Grande Museum has recently published a synthesis of more than a hundred years of archaeological research at the site, gleaned from various field notes and reports in its archives. The report, *Archaeology of the Pueblo Grande Platform Mound and Surrounding Features,* edited by Christian E. Downum, is available from the Pueblo Grande Museum. The data retrieved from both the excavations and archives will greatly augment what is known about Pueblo Grande.

The ruins are entered through the museum, which is adjacent to the platform mound and contains exhibits relating to historic and prehistoric Indian cultures of southern Arizona. An interpretive trail leads around and over the mound and gives visitors a view of a restored ball court. Unlike some Anasazi ruins, you have to use your imagination at Pueblo Grande to visualize how the site must have appeared seven or eight centuries ago. It is interesting to contemplate how history repeats itself. From the mound, you can view modern canals next to prehistoric ones and see how a modern city was built over the ruins of another long vanished.

Why did the residents of Pueblo Grande disappear? The Pima Indians have a story, passed down from person to person over the centuries. They say that the *Sivanyi* (Hohokam) offended their hero, Elder Brother, and even tried to kill him. In retaliation, the Pima and Tohono O'Odham (Papago) made war upon them and destroyed the Sivanyi villages, including Casa Grande and Pueblo Grande. Perhaps one day the Piman legend will be substantiated by the diggings of scientists.

The Pueblo Grande Museum is open from 9:00 A.M. to 4:45 P.M., Monday through Saturday, and from 1:00 to 4:45 P.M. on Sunday. There is an attractive picnic site along the Grand Canal next to the museum, and numerous hotels are located nearby.

> Suggested reading: *The Hohokam: Ancient People of the Desert*, edited by David Grant Noble, School of American Research Press, Santa Fe, New Mexico, 1991.

Casa Grande Ruins National Monument

Casa Grande Ruins National Monument is located on Arizona Highway 87, 1 mile north of Coolidge, Arizona. This is about midway between Phoenix and Tucson.

As a rule, the best preserved ruins were built of stone or lie in the shelter of caves. An exception can be found in Casa Grande, a massive, multistoried caliche-adobe house that has stood on an open plain, exposed to sun, wind, rain, and varying temperatures for more than six centuries. Its very existence today as more than just a mound on the desert flats testifies to the unique characteristics of this structure and the formidable construction effort put forth by its fourteenth-century builders.

Casa Grande is a ruin that has long perplexed archaeologists. What was it? The literature is replete with speculations on its original function—a chief's residence, storage house, temple or palace, administrative center, observatory for stargazers. Interpretations such as these are by no means mutually exclusive, and researchers today lean toward a view that an elite and regionally influential person, with both political and religious power, lived there.

The area around Casa Grande was occupied by Hohokam people who were highly successful agriculturalists with extensive irrigation systems and a widespread trading network. If a high priest or chief resided at Casa Grande, he would have had a view from his upper story of a large surrounding community,

Casa Grande.

as well as the lower section of the village's main canal, whose intake was sixteen miles up the Gila River. The peasant population over which he ruled would have lived in mud and stick huts surrounding his "big house." These huts melted into the desert soon after being abandoned. His own mansion was of a more puebloan style—it was possibly inspired by the architecture of the Anasazi to the north or by the Salado in the Tonto Basin. Scientists estimate that it was built in the early 1300s and used for only a few generations. It was the centerpiece of a village compound that contained many other residences and was surrounded by a high adobe wall.

The scientific record indicates that the Hohokam population declined in the Classic period (ca. A.D. 1100–1450) and that by the end of this period the culture had disappeared, at least in any archaeologically recognizable form. The people, however, carried on as desert dwellers, probably eventually to become the historic and contemporary Pima and Tohono O'Odham (Papago) tribes. But what happened to the Hohokam culture that was responsible for monumental sites like Casa Grande? Researchers are unable to shed much light on this key question. They speculate that a crop failure occurred, possibly resulting from waterlogged or salinized soils or from a major flood that destroyed the irrigation system. The Pima, however, tell stories passed down through the centuries of warfare between their ancestors and the Hohokam. According to their legend, they defeated the Hohokam and drove them out of their main towns, such as Casa Grande and Pueblo Grande.

As a building, Casa Grande represents the pinnacle of Hohokam-Pueblo architecture and village planning and has inspired generations of explorers and travelers. It was constructed principally of caliche earth, a desert subsoil with high lime content that becomes brick-hard. Building wood included ponderosa pine, white fir, juniper, and mesquite. The heavier timbers probably originated in mountain regions more than fifty miles distant, and the logs were probably floated down the Gila River. Over 600 roof beams were used, and at least 1,500 cubic yards of soil were set into the walls.

The walls of Casa Grande are deeply trenched in the ground. At their base, they are over four feet thick, but they taper to about two feet at full height. The mud was mixed to a thick consistency in holes in the ground, carried to the walls, and puddled by hand in courses about twenty-six inches high. Evidence of these courses is still clearly visible in wall cracking. The basic house was only two stories high, but it was built atop five feet of fill to give the structure greater height and dominance. A single third-story room was added that has a tunnel-like porthole in one wall, which

Hohokam vessel in Casa Grande museum.

aligns with the setting sun at summer solstice. Many southwestern Native American pueblos had similar calendrical features used by the sun priest to help schedule ceremonies.

A century and a half passed following the initial Spanish penetration into the Southwest before the first European, Jesuit missionary Eusebio Francisco Kino, laid eyes on Casa Grande. In 1694, Kino arrived in the Casa Grande area, guided by Sobaipuri Indians. The ruins became a landmark for subsequent exploratory expeditions as well as later travelers, frontiersmen, soldiers, settlers, and tourists. By 1880, the Southern Pacific Railroad had a station only twenty miles away from which regular tours were conducted to the site. The ruin had virtually no more protection from souvenir hunters and vandals than it did from the weather, and many artifacts and relics were carried off.

National interest in protecting Casa Grande began to crystalize following the 1887–1888 Hemenway Southwestern Archaeological Expedition, which included such distinguished anthropologists as Frank H. Cushing, J. Walter Fewkes, Adolph F. Bandelier, and Frederick W. Hodge. In 1892, 480 acres were set aside for the protection of the ruin, and the first shelter was erected eleven years later. In 1906–1907, Fewkes returned to conduct excavations and drainage and stabilization work, and in 1918, the site achieved national monument status.

An interpretive trail leads to the big house and other ruins within the Casa Grande village compound. Two hundred yards distant is the site of a ball court where "games" were probably attended by as many as 300 to 600 spectators. Today, the monument includes a picnic area, small desert botanical garden, bookshop, and museum with displays of Hohokam craft arts and tools. Visitors should plan to spend about an hour to see the museum and ruins. Food and lodging are available in nearby Coolidge and Florence, and several campgrounds are located in the vicinity, though not at the monument itself.

Suggested reading: *Casa Grande Ruins National Monument,* by Rose Houk, Southwest Parks and Monuments Association, Tucson, Arizona, 1987.

Painted Rocks Park

Painted Rocks Park is located near Gila Bend, Arizona. From Gila Bend, drive 30 miles west on Interstate 8 to the Painted Rocks exit and continue another 15 miles to the park.

Painted Rocks Park contains the heaviest concentration of petroglyphs in the Southwest. Here more than 750 images were pecked on smooth-faced basalt boulders that cover an isolated hill in this otherwise flat country. Historical records indicate that some of the glyphs were originally painted, hence the site name, which is translated from *Piedras Pintadas,* the name given to this place by early Spanish colonists.

The boulders at Painted Rocks contain an astounding array of pictures, including many human figures, animals, reptiles, and abstractions. Some images are of more recent origin, such as horses and riders. These later glyphs may have been made by Pima or Tohono O'Odham (Papago) Indians, who are thought to be today's descendents of the Hohokam. No one knows why the Indians chose this place for such intensive rock art. The boulder outcropping is a singular landmark along a route that was probably well traveled in ancient as well as modern times, and the rocks, with their dark desert varnish, lend themselves to glyph making. Perhaps the site had other significance as well, or was a periodic gathering place for local people.

Since there are no ruins in the close vicinity of the petroglyphs, their cultural affiliation is somewhat speculative. The Gila Bend region, however, was within the Hohokam cultural domain from about A.D. 700 to 1450, and most of the glyphs are similar

Petroglyphs at Painted Rocks Park.

in style—the Gila Petroglyph Style—to Hohokam rock art found to the east. Archaeological studies show that after A.D. 1100, the Gila Bend area also was influenced by the Patayan culture to the west, suggesting that for a period, at least, it was a contact zone between the Hohokam and Patayan peoples. Certainly, prehistoric and historic trade routes passed close by the site.

Until the Bureau of Land Management fenced off Painted Rocks in 1963, many of the smaller boulders with petroglyphs were carted off by people for frontyard landscaping. The fencing, while unsightly, provides needed security, and the site has seen little damage in recent years.

The nearest travel services are in the town of Gila Bend. Visitors may also be interested in seeing the ruins at Casa Grande Ruins National Monument (see p. 22) near Coolidge.

Suggested reading: "Hohokam, Patayan, or ?: Rock Art at Two Sites Near Gila Bend, Arizona," by Richard J. Martynec, *Rock Art Papers, Vol. 6,* edited by Ken Hedges, San Diego Museum Papers No. 24, San Diego, California, 1989.

The Hardy Site

The Hardy Site is located in Fort Lowell Park at 2900 North Craycroft Road in the northeast part of Tucson, Arizona.

First reported in 1884 by Adolph F. Bandelier, the Hardy Site contains the remains of a Hohokam village that once covered about a quarter of a square mile. Hohokam Indians lived here from about A.D. 300 to 1250. After they left, the elements collapsed and melted their houses onto the ground. In 1873, the United States Army built Fort Lowell directly upon the ancient Indian village. The adobe bricks made to construct the fort buildings contain potsherds and pieces of stone tools. Fort Lowell was abandoned in 1891, and eventually, the ancient Hohokam site beneath it was again disturbed by the construction of Tucson houses and apartments. In 1975, when Fort Lowell Park was being developed, an onlooker reported observing Hohokam artifacts in the construction site. His report led to archaeological excavations of a small portion of the site by the Arizona State Museum in the late 1970s. In 1979, the city opened an outdoor cultural exhibit in the park.

The archaeologists uncovered clusters of pithouses, trash mounds, outside roasting pits, caliche mining pits, work areas, and a cemetery and offeratory plaza. After completing their work, they backfilled the excavations to preserve them. Later, the city reconstructed a pithouse floor out of cement and erected a series of illustrated panels that depict various aspects of Hohokam life and culture. Except for a trash mound, there are no ruins to be viewed.

The Hohokam of the Tucson Basin were related culturally to other Hohokam people further north along the Gila and Salt rivers. They were attracted to the Tucson Basin for its richness in natural resources and long growing season. The basin is enclosed by five discontinuous mountain ranges from whose slopes sediments have eroded to collect in the valley. Along the floor of the valley flow streams that were used by the Hohokam for floodwater farming. Rather than create an extensive irrigation canal network, as did the Hohokam of the Phoenix Basin, these people utilized the flooding waters of streams, sometimes assisted by short ditches, to bring moisture to croplands situated close to the stream banks. This technique was especially effective in the rainy seasons of late winter and midsummer. According to reports written in the eighteenth and nineteenth centuries, these streams used to flow all year. Beavers built dams along them, and cottonwood and mesquite groves grew along their banks.

As the Hohokam became established in the Tucson Basin, agriculture evolved to be the mainstay of their economy. The residents at the Hardy Site took advantage of the fertile bottom-lands southwest of the confluence of Pantano Wash and Rillito Creek to raise corn, beans, and squash, and in their fields, they encouraged such edible weeds as pigweed, sunflower, and tansy mustard. They also raised cotton with which they wove such clothing as ponchos, shirts, and belts, and which they traded with their neighbors. This trade reached north to the Phoenix area and far east to the land of the Mogollon. In addition to farming, they also collected a wide variety of desert plants, seeds, and fruits. Visitors interested in this aspect of Hohokam life will enjoy Gary Nabhan's book, *Gathering the Desert* (University of Arizona Press, Tucson, Arizona, 1985). Plants were also gathered from the lower slopes of the Santa Catalina Mountains, and pine and fir trees on the higher slopes were chopped down to use in house building.

With the exception of platform mounds, some of which contain many thousands of cubic yards of fill, Hohokam sites generally leave meager "ruins." For the most part, the houses of these early people were single story and built of sticks and mud. Over time, they melted back into the desert, leaving traces that only are of interest to scientific researchers.

A factor that has played a role in the loss of Hohokam village sites is twentieth-century urbanization, and the Hardy Site is a good example of archaeological remains that have been overlaid by historic and modern development. The concession that Tucson has made here to cultural heritage can be seen in the painted panels, the cement pithouse floor, and an exhibit of Hohokam artifacts in the Fort Lowell Museum. To further your understanding of the Hohokam, a visit to the Arizona State Museum on the University of Arizona campus is recommended.

Suggested reading: *Hohokam Indians of the Tucson Basin,* by Linda M. Gregonis and Karl J. Reinhard, The University of Arizona Press, Tucson, Arizona, 1979.

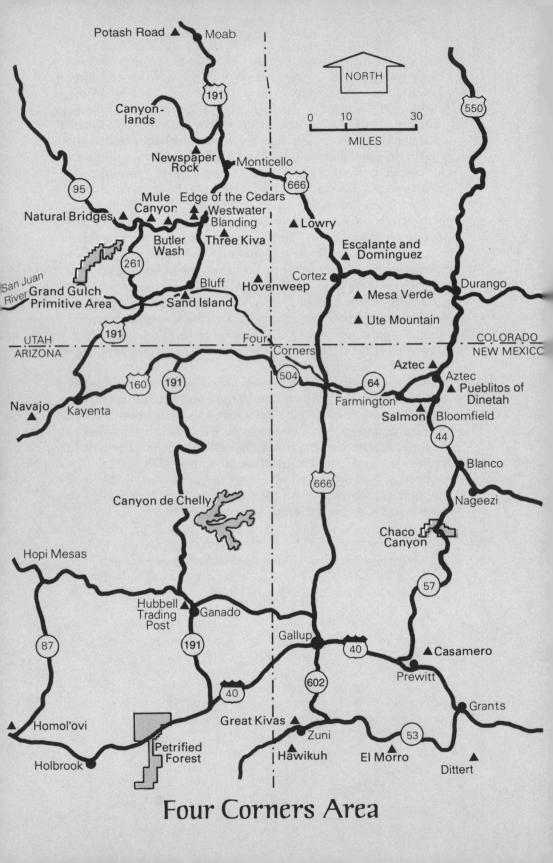

Four Corners Area

THE ANASAZI
A 2,000-Year Continuum

The prehistory of the American Southwest is dominated by one vital and enduring group of people—the Anasazi. This culture emerged in the first several centuries B.C. out of a seminomadic hunting and gathering tradition into a settled village life with an increasing dependence on horticulture. The first Anasazi sheltered themselves from the harsh winters of the Colorado Plateau in crude, shallow, one-family pithouses often built at the mouths of caves or under rock overhangs. Much later, the Anasazi acquired architectural and engineering skills with which they built large multistoried masonry pueblos, a few of which have survived in remarkably good condition to the present day.

Anasazi is a Navajo term often loosely translated as "Ancient Ones," but it can also connote an enemy people from the past. Despite frequent misleading inferences in popular literature, Anasazi ruins represent neither a vanished race nor a lost civilization. As one Anasazi descendant once commented, "After visiting the ruins of the Parthenon, do we conclude that the Greeks are extinct?"

Both as a people and to some degree as a culture, the former inhabitants of such places as Hawikuh (see p. 116), Sand Canyon (see p. 49), and Pecos (see p. 192) lived on to become the Pueblo Indians who now reside in parts of New Mexico and Arizona. Anyone attending a Hopi Niman kachina dance or a feast day at Taos or Santo Domingo will sense the spiritual legacy of the Anasazi, nurtured and modified over a hundred generations to emerge in contemporary culture. Over the generations, the Pueblo Indians have told and retold their origin story in the context of their religious traditions. This story also has been the subject of more than a century of study by archaeologists, who have attempted

Anasazi pictographs in Canyon de Chelly.

to reconstruct the past by looking at material culture, such as potsherds, spear points, and architecture. A pioneer in southwestern archaeology was Adolph F. Bandelier (1840–1914), after whom a national monument in New Mexico was named. He was succeeded by such prominent figures as Earl H. Morris, Alfred Vincent Kidder, A. E. Douglas, and Emil W. Haury. Today, the study is carried on by a new generation of scholars—W. James Judge, Linda S. Cordell, George J. Gumerman, and others of equal distinction.

In a hundred years, the tools of the archaeological trade have evolved from shovels and brooms to computers and high-tech dating methods, such as obsidian hydration and thermoluminescence. Today's methodology reflects an increasingly specialized and often less invasive approach than that of past decades. And yet, despite the fact that the Anasazi and other ancient southwesterners have been studied from nearly every conceivable angle, many important truths about their past have remained elusive.

From about 7,000 years ago to the time of Christ, the Southwest was inhabited by small scattered bands of people who moved frequently as they hunted small game and collected edible plants, seeds, nuts, and fruit. Over many centuries, these hunters and gatherers, who belonged to the Archaic or Desert culture, acquired a growing knowledge of and interest in how to control the plants they used. In addition, from their Mogollon neighbors to the south, they obtained seeds from an all-important domestic Mesoamerican grain known as maize or corn.

By the first few centuries B.C., these pre-Anasazi people found it increasingly advantageous (for reasons still not well understood) to abandon their nomadic ways in favor of a more sedentary communal existence. They cultivated corn, with beans and squash soon to follow, and began to live year-round in villages. This evolution marks the birth of Anasazi culture.

In discussing the stages of Anasazi cultural evolution over a two-millenia time span, archaeologists have developed a complex terminology, which most readers of this book may wish to ignore. However, since some temporal/cultural classifications appear repeatedly in museum exhibits and trail guides, the chart on page 34 may prove useful.

The earliest Anasazi are known as Basketmakers because of the many finely woven baskets found at their sites. Later, some of the functions of baskets were supplanted by ceramic vessels, and the Basketmakers, who lived in pithouses, began building above-ground masonry dwellings or pueblos. At this stage, archaeologists drop the term Basketmaker in favor of Pueblo. Both terms, however, refer to the Anasazi culture at earlier and later stages of development.

As they evolved, the Anasazi developed improved farming methods, invented many tools and utensils, and excelled in such endeavors as architecture, ceramics, basketry, weaving, and jewelry. They also increased in numbers and expanded over a large territory. Within this territory, archaeologists have identified three main Anasazi cultural districts: the Chacoan (centered at Chaco Canyon, New Mexico); the Mesa Verdean or Northern San Juan (centered around present-day Cortez, Colorado); and the Kayenta (centered around Kayenta, Arizona, and Navajo National Monument). The religious practices of the Anasazi became elaborate and their social organization grew complex. They also traded extensively with other Indians who lived as far away as

Anasazi mug at Edge of the Cedars museum.

	ANASAZI	CHRONOLOGY	
Date	Pecos Classification	Robert's Classification	Characteristics and Events
200 B.C.– A.D. 450	Basketmaker I Basketmaker II	Basketmaker	Hunters and gatherers turning to horticulture. Habitations in caves. Atlatl in use. No pottery. Basketry.
450–700	Basketmaker III	Modified Basketmaker	Pithouse villages. Pottery made. Bow and arrow in use.
700–900 900–1100	Pueblo I Pueblo II	Developmental Pueblo	Above-ground pueblos. Pithouse becomes kiva. Cotton in use.
1100–1300	Pueblo III	Great Pueblo	Population expansion in uplands. Advances in agriculture, architecture, crafts. Developed complex socio-religious organization. Cliff dwellings.
1300–1700	Pueblo IV	Regressive Pueblo	Resettlement in new areas. Social and economic change.
1700–present	Pueblo V	Historic Pueblo	Strong influence from European culture. Much social, cultural, economic change. Some traditions continue.

southern Mexico and the Pacific Coast. Anasazi culture reached a true flowering in the twelfth and thirteenth centuries (the Pueblo III or Great Pueblo period), especially along the San Juan River and its tributaries. The influence of the culture spread farther afield, as can be seen in the building style at Casa Grande (see p. 22) and Gila Cliff Dwellings (see p. 5).

The bust that followed this boom began in the mid-1100s at Chaco Canyon and a century later in the northern San Juan region around Mesa Verde. At these times, the Anasazi abandoned their San Juan/Four Corners homeland. Some went south to the Hopi Mesas, others to the Little Colorado River and the Zuni Mountains, and still others to the Rio Grande valley far to the east. These migrations sometimes took several generations to complete. What brought about these changes is a major unresolved question in Anasazi studies. Climate change is the most cited

Pueblo deer dancers.

cause and, to be sure, the Southwest did experience intense drought between 1275 and 1299, when migrations were most intense. Drought, however, probably was not the only reason. Soil erosion and the consequent lowering of water tables may have hampered irrigation in some areas. Depletion of natural resources, such as game and wood, may also have been reasons, and disease should not be discounted. In another realm, political or religious factionalism may have brought about schisms within specific communities, a common occurance in historic times.

Some scholars have suggested that by the mid-1500s, Pueblo culture was experiencing a resurgence that may have carried it beyond its former florescence. Certainly, some Pueblo communities were attaining a size and complexity rivaling that of the major San Juan centers. But in 1540, when Francisco de Coronado stormed the Zuni pueblo of Hawikuh (see p. 116), a new era of Anasazi-Pueblo history began. In the early 1600s, Pueblo Indians saw the introduction of an awesome new war technology, diseases to which they had no immunity, a militant foreign religion, and a dominant European civil authority.

Under Spanish colonization, the Pueblo world changed more rapidly than in any previous period. Pueblo population declined, and the Spanish concentrated many of their scattered communities around Franciscan missions. The Spaniards imposed their own administrative system on the Pueblos, and their Christianizing efforts, including the suppression of some native religious practices, had a profound and lasting effect on Indian culture. Still, many Indian traditions continued. Using stone, adobe, and wood, the

Anasazi and their Pueblo descendants built beautifully designed communal houses that blended aesthetically with the environment. The finest examples from prehistory can be seen at Pueblo Bonito in Chaco Canyon and Cliff Palace at Mesa Verde. The tradition is still evident today at the Taos, Acoma, and Hopi pueblos.

Pueblo religion, with its rich mythology, elaborate ceremonialism, and special world view, survived too, despite repression by Spanish overlords. Today, at many Rio Grande villages, native Pueblo and Christian rituals are practiced side by side, as it were, in the church and in the kiva. Still another ancestral connection can be seen in native Pueblo languages, which continue to be spoken on most reservations.

The descendants of the Anasazi, then, have integrated two worlds. A computer programmer at Los Alamos or salesperson at Sears may invest much time throughout the year practicing religious rituals that have survived from Anasazi roots. A visit to Zuni is more poignant when you wander through the ruins of Atsinna (see p. 113) or Hawikuh (see p. 116); likewise, a tour of Poshuouinge (see p. 184) has more meaning after meeting the people from San Juan or Santa Clara pueblos, whose ancestors lived at these sites.

Suggested reading: *The Anasazi,* by J. J. Brody, Rizzoli, New York, New York, 1990; *Prehistory of the Southwest,* by Linda S. Cordell, Academic Press, San Diego, California, 1984.

Mesa Verde National Park

The entrance to Mesa Verde National Park is along U.S. 160, just east of Cortez and 34 miles west of Durango, Colorado. From the park entrance to the headquarters and museum is an additional 21 slow-driving miles.

Far above me, a thousand feet or so, set in a great cavern in the face of the cliff, I saw a little city of stone asleep. It was as still as sculpture—and something like that. It all hung together, seemed to have a kind of composition: pale little houses of stone nestling close to one another, perched on top of each other, with flat roofs, narrow windows, straight walls, and in the middle of the group, a round tower. . . .

In the sunlight it was the colour of winter oak leaves. A fringe of cedars grew along the edge of the cavern, like a garden. They were the only living things. Such silence

Cliff Palace, Mesa Verde National Park.

and stillness and repose—immortal repose. That village sat looking down into the canyon with the calmness of eternity. . . . I had come upon the city of some extinct civilization, hidden away in this inaccessible mesa for centuries, preserved in the dry air and almost perpetual sunlight like a fly in amber, guarded by the cliffs and the river and the desert.

Willa Cather
The Professor's House

Some have called Mesa Verde the Disneyland of American archaeology. Its many cliff dwellings set in great open rock alcoves create a feeling of fantasy and romance and seem more the invention of a Hollywood set designer than the remnants of 700-year-old Indian villages.

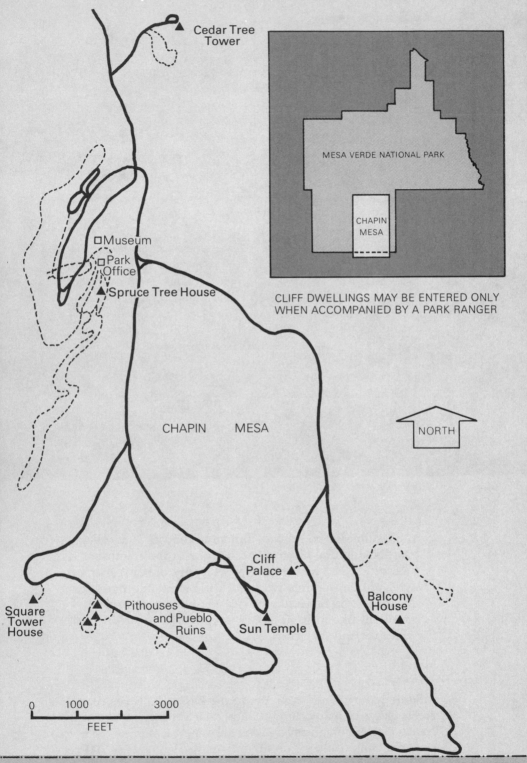

Cedar Tree
Tower

MESA VERDE NATIONAL PARK

CHAPIN
MESA

CLIFF DWELLINGS MAY BE ENTERED ONLY
WHEN ACCOMPANIED BY A PARK RANGER

Museum
Park
Office
Spruce Tree House

CHAPIN   MESA

NORTH

Cliff
Palace

Balcony
House

Square
Tower
House

Pithouses
and Pueblo
Ruins

Sun Temple

0   1000   3000

FEET

UTE MOUNTAIN INDIAN RESERVATION

Mesa Verde National Park

To Richard Wetherill, the Mancos rancher who "discovered" these ruins (long known by the Ute Indians), Mesa Verde was a rough wilderness in which no sensible cowboy would want to lose track of his cows. But today, that wild mesa is tamed, and streams of summer tourists from around the world park their cars and campers at the scenic overlooks, follow guides along paved walkways to stabilized cliff dwellings, and enjoy the conveniences of a modern resort. From a once remote, almost forbidding wilderness where underbrush, cliffs, and labyrinthine canyons made passage all but impossible, Mesa Verde has developed into the most popular archaeological preserve in North America. Six hundred thousand people visit annually.

Wetherill, after exploring and digging many of these sites, dedicated much of his later life to searching out Anasazi ruins in other parts of the Southwest. He excavated vast amounts of pre-Columbian artifacts, many in fine condition, but was frustrated and disappointed by the apathetic response, from lay people and scholars alike, to his discoveries. Were he alive today, he would no doubt be astounded by the overwhelming attention modern generations bestow upon his beloved cliff dwellings.

Although a few Archaic projectile points, dating from 1000 to 3000 B.C. have been found on Mesa Verde, the earliest recorded human habitations on the mesa are much later—about A.D. 600. These are Basketmaker villages consisting of half a dozen or so pithouses that sheltered an equal number of extended families. The relatively late date of these sites is curious, since many similar sites in the lowlands surrounding Mesa Verde are much older. Apparently, it took the early Anasazi a long time to discover Mesa Verde.

Why did they choose to live here? The mesa and its climate, which has changed little since then, had many advantages: good annual rainfall, timber for building houses, wood for fuel, warmer temperatures than in the Mancos Valley below, and fertile soils. Mesa Verde had numerous other essential resources, such as nutritious and medicinal plants, abundant game, reliable springs, and the materials for manufacturing tools and household utensils.

Beginning about A.D. 750, the Mesa Verdeans began living in above-ground, "wattle and daub" structures. These living and storage rooms were made of upright posts, woven through with slender branches, and coated with mud. They were quick and easy shelters but provided little protection from the bitter winds and snows of Colorado winters. Perhaps for this reason, the Indians soon began building small contiguous masonry rooms, which eventually evolved into full-fledged pueblos. Still, they kept making the pithouses, using them for ceremonial purposes.

Visitors often assume all Mesa Verdeans lived in cliff dwellings but, in truth, most lived in open villages on the mesa tops. An example is Far View House, which was first settled about A.D. 900 and by 1100 housed some 500 people. This site is open to the public.

It was not until about A.D. 1200 that many people moved off the mesas to build Mesa Verde's renowned cliff dwellings. They chose as building sites the vaulted shallow caves and rock overhangs in Cliff and Fewkes canyons. By the mid-1200s, these cliff dwellings housed about half the population of Chapin Mesa. The new villages were somewhat isolated from each other, but their occupants would have met frequently along the trails to springs, on hunting and gathering forays, and occasionally at ceremonies at Sun Temple and Fire Temple, which tourists also can visit.

Mesa Verdeans only lived in their cliff dwellings—Cliff Palace, Spruce Tree House, Balcony House, Long House, and many others—for less than a century. Why did they move to these sites? Archaeologists have long debated this question. The sites seem defensive, but who was the enemy, and where is the evidence of fighting? For a lucid and fuller discussion of cliff dwellings, refer to the suggested reading list, Jeffrey S. Dean's essay in particular.

It is believed that some Mesa Verde families began to trickle away from the mesa as early as the mid-1100s, with this gradual flow continuing until the massive exodus in the late 1200s. The final word has yet to be written on why they left, but a severe drought between 1275 and 1299 probably motivated the main exodus. Compounding the drought were environmental depletions, including deer, timber, and firewood. The Mesa Verdeans were eating squirrels and rabbits rather than large game. Scarcities of food and fuel resources may have had an impact on the health and vigor of the population, setting up conditions in which drought would have been disastrous.

Other theories explaining Mesa Verde's abandonment also have been suggested, such as internal factionalism, external attack, disease, and a lowering of the birth rate. None of these ideas are mutually exclusive; they all could be spin-offs of the original drought/environment hypothesis.

In recent decades, new discoveries have put Mesa Verde in new perspective. It seems the population of the Montezuma Valley, north of Cortez, far exceeded that of Mesa Verde. In fact, Mesa Verde, with an estimated peak population of about 2,500, was no larger than Yellow Jacket, only one of eight major pueblos in the valley.

After A.D. 1300, Mesa Verde was virtually deserted, and as Willa Cather eloquently writes in her novel, the cliff dwellings long

Square Tower House, Mesa Verde National Park.

Classic black-on-white kiva jar. Chapin Mesa Museum, Mesa Verde National Park.

lay silent. The numerous archaeological studies focused on Mesa Verde sites can be largely explained by public fascination with romantic cliff dwellings and lack of interest in the more pedestrian looking mounds that lie among the pinto bean fields of the Montezuma Valley. A few of the people who contributed to Mesa Verde archaeological studies are Gustav Nordenskiold, Jesse L. Nusbaum, Jesse Walter Fewkes, James A. Lancaster, Douglas Osborne, Alden C. Hayes, and Arthur H. Rohn. Their reports would fill a bookcase.

Mesa Verde National Park has a fine museum at the visitor center on Chapin Mesa where you can learn which ruins are open and when guided tours are offered. The schedule changes seasonally. Spruce Tree House, an outstanding cliff village below the museum, is always open.

The twelve-mile Ruins Road includes two driving loops that pass a series of mesa-top pithouses and pueblo ruins as well as cliff-house overlooks. Self-guided and guided tours are available to several of the best ruins. Many are open in the summer during the peak tourist season but are closed off season. Depending on season and weather, tours may be offered to Step House, Long House, and other sites on Wetherill Mesa. Cliff Palace, the largest cliff dwelling in the Southwest with more than 200 rooms and 23 kivas, is a place you will never forget. Even when closed, it can be viewed from an observation point.

In summer, the Park Service holds campfire talks at Morefield campground (usually open from 1 June to 29 September) and offers nature walks to children. Far View Lodge on Chapin Mesa is a good place to stay (though it is closed in winter) and has a restaurant. There is also a nearby cafeteria. In addition, the park has a gas station, general store, laundromat, and snackbar. Most concessions are only open from mid-May to mid-October. Visitors can find other travel facilities in Mancos, Cortez, and Durango.

Mesa Verde National Park is a true archaeological and natural wonder. Its charms, however, are somewhat compromised in the summer by the large numbers of visitors. People wishing to see Mesa Verdean cliff dwellings in a quieter atmosphere should visit off season or consider taking a tour of the sites in Ute Mountain Tribal Park (see below).

> Suggested reading: *Understanding the Anasazi of Mesa Verde and Hovenweep,* Ancient City Press, Santa Fe, New Mexico, 1992. "Tse Yaa Kin: Houses Beneath the Rock," by Jeffrey S. Dean, in *Canyon de Chelly and Navajo National Monument,* Ancient City Press, Santa Fe, New Mexico, 1986.

Ute Mountain Tribal Park

Ute Mountain Tribal Park is located along the Mancos Canyon near Cortez, Colorado. The Ute Mountain Tribe conducts half-day, full-day, and special group tours to the Indian ruins and rock art sites on a year-round basis. The tours, for which there is a fee, are by advance reservation only (call 303-565-3751, ext. 282). They depart at 9 A.M. from the Ute Mountain Pottery Factory in Towaoc, 12 miles south of Cortez on U.S. 666.

When European-American settlers first came to southwestern Colorado, the region was the traditional territory of the Ute Indians. Today, the Utes administer Ute Mountain Tribal Park, which covers 125,000 acres within their reservation. The park encompasses the Mancos River Canyon into which drain the famous cliff-dwelling canyons of Mesa Verde. Ute Mountain Park has been called "the other Mesa Verde" because it too contains a wealth of Anasazi cliff and pueblo ruins as well as numerous Anasazi and Ute rock art sites. It is fitting that the thousands of archaeological sites here are in the custody of Native Americans whose ancestors roamed this land many generations ago.

The Anasazi ruins in the park share the same cultural history as those adjacent in Mesa Verde National Park. For a more detailed discussion of the Mesa Verde Anasazi, see page 36.

Although these twin parks share the same cultural history, the experience of visiting their ruins is entirely different. The heavy tourism and commercialism of Mesa Verde National Park (600,000 visitors per year) is absent. Here, the cliff dwellings and their

Eagle Nest, Ute Mountain Tribal Park.

environment remain in a relatively pristine, unrestored state. Experiencing the sites in a small group, at a relaxed pace, in the company of a Ute Indian guide has an altogether different quality.

The standard half-day tour covers ruins and rock art sites within scenic lower Mancos Canyon; the full-day tour continues on to the upper tributary canyons to view or hike to a variety of cliff dwellings. Johnson Canyon alone contains more than thirty dwellings, and at Lion Canyon, a one-and-a-half-mile rustic, cliffside trail leads to a series of cliff houses: Tree House, Lion House, Morris V, and Eagle Nest. At these sites, visitors can linger to enjoy canyon panoramas and take pictures; walk in and around many rooms; pick up (and put down) ancient potsherds, corncobs, and tool fragments; and converse with the guide.

Mancos Canyon was first surveyed in 1874 by a small offshoot party of the famous Hayden Expedition. Ferdinand V. Hayden was exploring the Rocky Mountains and had just mapped Yellowstone National Park and the Tetons. Hayden sent his photographer, William Henry Jackson, ahead with a small party, and while outfitting in Denver, Jackson heard a tale about abandoned cliff houses in the rough canyon country of southwestern Colorado. His imagination piqued, he went on to investigate. One evening, after a long day's ride, Jackson and his group were camped in lower Mancos Canyon, discouraged that their arduous travels had not yet confirmed the story. Then, one member looked up and spotted "something that appeared very much like a house." The following day, they climbed up to the ruins, and with his heavy 11- by 14-inch view camera and glass plate negatives, Jackson made the first photograph of a Mesa Verde cliff dwelling. The site, which he named Two Story Cliff Dwelling, can be seen today on a tour of Ute Mountain Tribal Park.

A site along the Mancos Canyon road contains a visually stunning panel of Ute pictographs, including depictions in red paint of human faces and figures, horses and riders, and a horse's head. Next to this site once stood the dwelling of Chief Jack House, the last traditional chief of the Ute Mountain Tribe, who died in 1971 at the age of eighty-six. Since his death, the tribe has been governed by an elected chairman and council.

To visit Ute Mountain Park is a special experience but not recommended for travelers desiring the amenities of the adjacent national park. Although the Ute Tribe plans to obtain a van, it is presently necessary to drive your own car on the tour. For the full-day tour, this involves about eighty miles of driving on dusty gravel and dirt roads. You must also bring along drinking water and lunch and be prepared for hiking on rough trails up and down wooden ladders. Although this is the charm of the experience, it is not for everyone.

The Ute Mountain Tribe also offers custom tours of the park for people interested in camping, multiday backpacking hikes, or rock climbing. Package tours that include transportation, meals, and equipment, however, are not presently available. Whatever type of trip you design, you are responsible for everything you need and must hire a guide.

Nearby Cortez offers many travel services, or arrangements can be made to stay at a tribal campground in the park. Other archaeological parks and sites in the vicinity include Hovenweep National Monument (see p. 51), the Escalante and Dominguez ruins (see following pages), and Lowry Pueblo Ruins (see p. 55).

Suggested reading: *Ute Mountain Tribal Park: The Other Mesa Verde*, by Jean Akens, Four Corners Publications, Moab, Utah, 1987. *People of the Shining Mountains*, by Charles S. Marsh, Pruett Publishing Company, Boulder, Colorado, 1982.

Anasazi Heritage Center

The Anasazi Heritage Center, 3 miles west of Dolores, Colorado, on Colorado 184, includes the Escalante and Dominguez ruins. The center is 18 miles north of the entrance to Mesa Verde National Park.

Today, when federal lands are to be disturbed, legislation requires that an environmental impact study be conducted, which includes a study of archaeological resources that might be damaged. This process, though long and costly, has funded research at many archaeological sites. In 1968, the federal government authorized construction of a major irrigation dam that eventually flooded hundreds of archaeological sites in the Dolores Valley. The decision to dam the Dolores River initiated the largest archaeological research project in American history. Cofunded by the Bureau of Reclamation and the Bureau of Land Management, archaeologists located more than 1,600 sites, tested 125, and studied a wealth of data. In addition, the Anasazi Heritage Center, which oversees the Escalante and Dominguez ruins, was created.

The ruins were named for two Spanish friars who encamped nearby in 1776 and discovered the Escalante site. They had left Santa Fe sixteen days before to seek a new route to Monterey, California. Excavations at the Escalante Ruins were conducted with American Bicentennial funds on the 200th anniversary of this Spanish expedition.

The Escalante Ruin is a twenty-room masonry pueblo situated on a hill above the Anasazi Heritage Center and overlooking McPhee Reservoir. To the south, the low ridgeline of Mesa Verde lies darkly on the horizon. Archaeologists believe Escalante Pueblo was built about A.D. 1129 by Anasazi immigrants from Chaco Canyon in northwestern New Mexico (see p. 119), and was occupied, except for two short periods of abandonment, until the early 1200s. Then, as today, the environment offered a variety of food resources, materials for building, tool and pottery manufacture, and an abundance of water. Mule deer, antelope, elk, and bighorn sheep also enjoyed the plentiful resources of the area and provided meat for the Anasazi. Additionally, the site sat along a trade route, which helped keep its residents in contact with near and distant neighbors.

Two elements immediately identify Escalante Pueblo as a Chacoan outlier. First is its characteristically Chacoan layout—a large rectangular preplanned room block, with living and storage rooms, enclosing a central kiva. Second, the walls have dressed exterior stones and a rubble and mud core. Like numerous other Chacoan outliers, the site sat atop a hill or ridge looking down on many smaller surrounding hamlets.

Escalante Ruins near the Anasazi Heritage Center.

If Escalante's architecture is Chacoan, other cultural remains at the site, such as pottery, reflect a strong Mesa Verdean (or Northern San Juan Anasazi) influence. Archaeologists have suggested an intriguing prehistoric scenario. A group of men moved here from the Chaco area to the south to establish a trading post. They built the pueblo in their own style and married local women, who made pottery in the Mesa Verdean style. Possibly, the people at Escalante Pueblo even spoke different native tongues; and yet, they shared responsibilities and raised intertribal families. Their marital ties probably also had political and economic implications.

The Dominguez Ruin, next to the Anasazi Heritage Center's parking lot, is one of several lesser Mesa Verdean sites surrounding the hill. It has only four rooms and probably was the home of an extended family about A.D. 1123. Though unimpressive visually, it contained one exciting find—a "high status burial." A dead woman, about thirty-five years of age, was interred with an impressive collection of jewelry (including 6,900 beads) and other artifacts. Archaeologists have found very few such burials anywhere in the Southwest, which has given rise to a prevailing notion that Anasazi society was egalitarian. Of course, a future researcher may surprise everyone by discovering that the Anasazi buried their elite in some special manner that left no physical traces for archaeologists to find.

The Anasazi Heritage Center, which manages the ruins, is a new museum dedicated to the Anasazi culture. Its fine exhibits draw heavily on the material excavated during the course of the Dolores Archaeological Program, including the grave goods from the Dominguez Ruin. Of special note is a rotating display of Anasazi craft from the superb Chappell collection. A full-size replica of a late-800s Anasazi pithouse is also on display, which is based on a nearby site excavated in the 1980s.

The center includes more than displays; it stores almost two million artifacts and documents from prior research work and includes a research laboratory, library, theater, conference rooms, and excellent bookshop focusing on Native American culture. One innovative section of the museum, the "Discovery Room," includes a hands-on archaeological laboratory complete with microscope and computer displays and storage cabinets filled with Anasazi tools that visitors can pick up and handle.

The Anasazi Heritage Center has all the modern conveniences needed by travelers. You may wish to see the museum first, then follow the path to the ruins, which takes about fifteen minutes. The towns of Dolores and Cortez both have travel and tourist facilities, and you can find camping and fishing sites along the shores of the reservoir. Nearby archaeological areas include Mesa Verde (see p. 36), Hovenweep (see p. 51), Lowry (see p. 55), Sand Canyon (opposite), and Ute Mountain Park (see p. 43).

Suggested reading: *The Archaeology and Stabilization of the Dominguez and Escalante Ruins*, Colorado State Office, Bureau of Land Management, Denver, Colorado, 1979.

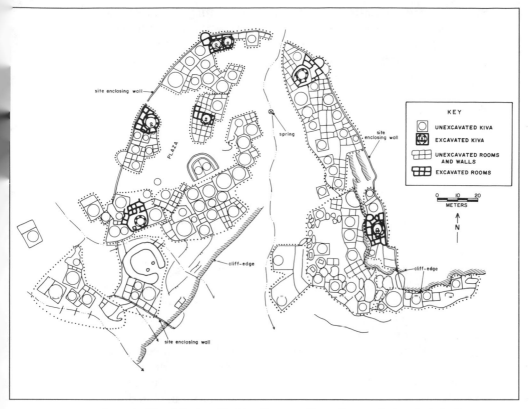

Layout of Sand Canyon Pueblo. Courtesy Crow Canyon Archaeological Center.

Sand Canyon Pueblo

Sand Canyon Pueblo is located off U.S. 666, a short distance northwest of Cortez, Colorado. The site is open to the public but access is controlled to protect the ruins. For further information and directions to the site, call the Bureau of Land Management in Durango at (303) 247-4082.

Sand Canyon Pueblo is a major Anasazi village dating to the latter part of the thirteenth century. The ruins surround a spring at the head of a tributary to Sand Canyon, which is part of the larger McElmo drainage. In its heyday, Sand Canyon Pueblo was a significant population and ritual center in the area. Its estimated 725 residents lived in pueblo-style dwellings around the edge of the canyon in what appears to have been a tightly knit community. The village consisted of 420 rooms, 90 kivas, 14 towers, an enclosed plaza, and other structures.

The Crow Canyon Archaeological Center, which is located near the site, has been conducting an in-depth research program at

Sand Canyon, including an innovative educational and public participation dimension. Through the program, lay people with an interest in archaeology and southwestern cultural history can enroll in a variety of anthropological workshops and seminars and assist in both field and laboratory work. Visitors wishing more information on this program should contact Crow Canyon Archaeological Center, 23390 County Road K, Cortez, Colorado 81321 or call 1-800-422-8975.

Crow Canyon's findings regarding Sand Canyon Pueblo suggest that the village's overall layout was preplanned by its builders and inhabitants. One clue to this preplanning is the existence of a massive enclosing stone wall that was constructed prior to the residences and public buildings within. The building of this wall must have been a major community project; estimates are that a work force of thirty-six people could have done the job in about two months.

Architecturally, archaeologists see the village as a series of fourteen room blocks, each consisting of groups of residential and storage rooms associated with a kiva. While these room blocks were part of the overall preplanned design, they were built and added onto as needed.

Sand Canyon Pueblo's east side appears to have been more residential in character than its west side. From their homes, the east-side residents would have had a good view across the canyon to the west side of the village with its more public areas and buildings. The west side, for example, had a community plaza, which was probably used for public events, such as dances, as well as a greater number of kivas, a possible great kiva, and other public structures. The large number of kivas at Sand Canyon indicates the degree to which these agriculturalists incorporated religion and ceremonialism into their lives and suggests that the village probably played an important ritual role in a larger community.

Crow Canyon Archaeological Center plans to continue its research at Sand Canyon Pueblo through the 1990s, using the site as an archaeological laboratory to help reconstruct a picture of Northern San Juan Anasazi cultural history in the late thirteenth century. Researchers will be investigating the significance of the site's apparent master plan, which has interesting parallels to the planning of Chacoan sites. They also will be studying how Sand Canyon related to other sites in the vicinity. But perhaps the most significant problem they will study here concerns the abandonment. Why did the Anasazi leave Sand Canyon in the late 1200s? Ongoing research may shed more light on this question, which is connected to the abandonment of the entire Four Corners region and has intrigued archaeologists for many years.

The Bureau of Land Management, in cooperation with Crow

Canyon, maintains a rustic interpretive trail that meanders through the ruins. For reasons of preservation, the excavations are being backfilled after excavation, so there is little to see beyond pueblo mounds and room outlines. Also, the site is heavily wooded, which inhibits the views across the village and over the canyon that its original inhabitants must have enjoyed. For this reason, Sand Canyon Pueblo is of more interest to people with a serious archaeological curiosity than to casual tourists. Individuals or groups wishing a guided tour of the site should contact Crow Canyon Archaeological Center in advance to inquire about possible arrangements. From late May to mid-October, the center offers one-day programs that include a laboratory tour and visit to working excavation sites.

Cortez offers many travel services, and readers may wish to visit other nearby ruins at Hovenweep (see below), Mesa Verde (see p. 36), Anasazi Heritage Center (see p. 46), and Ute Mountain Tribal Park (see p. 43).

Suggested reading: *The Anasazi*, by J. Richard Ambler, Museum of Northern Arizona, Flagstaff, Arizona, 1977.

Hovenweep National Monument

Hovenweep National Monument straddles the Colorado-Utah border west of Cortez, Colorado. Monument headquarters are located at Square Tower Group on the mostly unpaved road between Pleasant View, Colorado, 25 miles to the northeast, and Hatch Trading Post, 16 miles to the west in Utah. Directions to the monument are well marked along the roads.

Hovenweep, which means "deserted valley" in Ute, has a poetic sound that almost suggests the desolate canyons and barren mesas of the area. Viewing this landscape today, which supports only range cattle and a few scattered Navajo homesteads, we wonder how it could have sustained a vigorous population of Anasazi farmers.

Hovenweep National Monument actually consists of six clusters of ruins, four in Colorado and two in Utah. The ancient buildings usually are situated at the heads of draws which drain into lower McElmo Creek and the San Juan River. Visitors can walk from the monument headquarters to several sites in Square Tower Canyon. Other groups of ruins—Holly, Horseshoe, Hackberry, Cajon, and Cutthroat Castle—can be reached by driving several miles on unpaved roads, then hiking short distances.

Paleo-Indians wandered through the Hovenweep country as

long as 14,000 years ago as they traveled about in search of big game. During the Archaic period, which preceded that of the Anasazi, hunter-gatherers also used the mesas and canyons on their seasonal rounds. It was not until about A.D. 500 or so that the Anasazi—part of the Mesa Verde branch—began to settle here. Fifteen centuries ago, when the region had deeper soils and better foraging potential than it does today, a few Hovenweep villages were scattered on the mesa ridges and surrounding flatlands. They must have thrived, for after A.D. 750, the population tripled and it continued to grow after A.D. 900.

About 1150, the Hovenweep inhabitants began building larger pueblos around fortress-like stone towers at the heads of box canyons. In these locations, moisture that had percolated through the porous sandstone on the mesas to an impervious underlying layer of shale flowed laterally underground to emerge at the canyon heads in the form of seeps and springs. The Indians built check dams and reservoirs to better control this water supply and the floodwaters that occasionally spilled over the canyon rims. By such methods, they managed to cultivate garden plots of corn, beans, and squash on the terraced slopes of the lower canyons and to encourage the growth of other native edible or useful plants, such as beeweed, ground cherry, sedges, milkweed, cattail, and wolf berry. Their long tradition of hunting and foraging also helped supplement their diet.

Encircling the canyon heads, the Hovenweep people built massive stone pueblos, understandably referred to as "castles" by nineteenth-century explorers. And within the canyons, often just below the spring, they built tall stone towers, the principal purpose of which is not fully known. The square, oval, circular, and D-shaped towers exhibit expert masonry skills and engineering. Foundation leveling was often ignored by these builders, some of whose structures were (and still are) perched firmly on massive uneven chunks of fallen rimrock. The towers are a true enigma. Except for some narrow peepholes, they are virtually windowless and at least one has no door; it must have been entered from the roof, which was reached by ladder.

The towers of Hovenweep stand like timeless sentinels of a long-forgotten treasure. Many people have speculated as to their function. Did they guard the precious springs? Were they lookouts? Signal towers? Forts? Celestial observatories? Granaries? Water reservoirs? Habitations? Ceremonial innovations? It will be exciting if some future researchers learn their true significance.

The Indians left their Hovenweep pueblos in the late 1200s

Holly Group, Hovenweep National Monument.

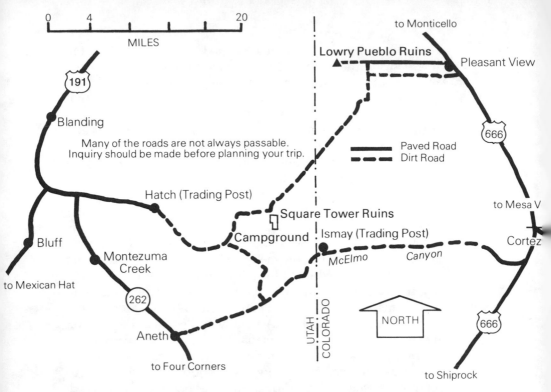

Hovenweep National Monument

never to return. At the same time, the entire Four Corners region was being abandoned by the Anasazi, possibly in response to a regional drought. It is believed that many Northern San Juan Anasazi moved south and east to the Little Colorado River drainage and the valley of the Rio Grande. But such migrations are hard to trace after a long time span. Wherever they went and for whatever reasons, they left behind truly impressive monuments to remember them by. These monuments, which have endured fire, rain, snow, wind, and vandals, are a tribute to the Hovenweep architects.

In 1854, a Mormon expedition first saw the Hovenweep ruins, which were well known to local Utes. Sixty-five years later, the Smithsonian Institution published Jesse Walter Fewkes's *Prehistoric Villages, Castles, and Towers of Southwestern Colorado*, which described the sites. Since Fewkes's survey report, surprisingly little research has been conducted here, although in the 1970s, limited investigations were carried out by the Hovenweep Archaeological Project, under the direction of Joseph C. Winter and others.

Hovenweep is a geographically disconnected monument. Visitors should stop first at the small visitor center at Square

Tower Group, which is the largest and best preserved complex of ruins. The trail from here passes Hovenweep Castle, Hovenweep House, Square Tower, Talus Pueblo, and other archaeological and environmental features. The hike takes about an hour. Directions to other outlying ruins are available at the visitor center.

A couple of precautions are worth noting. If you plan to drive to the outlying ruins, check weather conditions as roads in this area become slippery when wet. Remember how vulnerable these ruins are; visitors have been known to scale the walls of some of the ruins, knocking off building stones in the process. Finally, if you wander through these canyons, keep an eye out for snakes, especially if you have small children.

Hovenweep has romantic ruins, small picturesque canyons, and relatively few visitors and is easy to reach from Cortez, Bluff, or Blanding. If you wish to stay here longer, the campground has fresh water and modern toilet facilities but no food or firewood.

Suggested reading: "Hovenweep Through Time," by Joseph C. Winter, in *Understanding the Anasazi of Mesa Verde and Hovenweep,* edited by David Grant Noble, School of American Research, Santa Fe, New Mexico, 1985.

Lowry Pueblo Ruins

Lowry Pueblo Ruins are in southwestern Colorado near the town of Pleasant View on U.S. 666. At Pleasant View, turn west and proceed 9 miles, following road signs to the site.

The county road from Pleasant View to Lowry Pueblo Ruins meanders through rolling hills and vales with pinto bean fields stretching in all directions. The land is as fertile, well watered, and productive today as it was centuries ago when the Anasazi farmed here.

Lowry Pueblo was one of eight major Anasazi towns that dotted the Montezuma Valley (north of present-day Cortez) after A.D. 1100. Some of these towns had populations larger than the combined Cliff Canyon/Fewkes Canyon villages on Mesa Verde. The largest town, Yellow Jacket, reached a maximum size of 1,800 rooms and an estimated 2,500 people. This site, which is not open to the public, has been excavated in recent years by the University of Colorado, and a portion of it is owned and protected by the Archaeological Conservancy. Still another town was Sand Canyon Pueblo (see p. 49), which is also being excavated.

Archaeologists have traditionally referred to the people who lived in the northern Anasazi territory as "Mesa Verdeans" because aspects of their culture resembled that of Mesa Verde with which they were so familiar. But today it is generally recognized that the largest concentration of Mesa Verdean population was in the Montezuma Valley rather than on the mesa itself. As you travel to various sites, you will notice that interpretive signs refer to their former occupants both as the Northern San Juan Anasazi and as Mesa Verdeans. Do not be confused, they are one and the same. The change in terminology reflects the fact that Mesa Verde itself, with its spectacular cliff dwellings, is no longer viewed as the center of this Anasazi subculture.

Although parts of Lowry date much earlier, the main town was built after A.D. 1060. As its population grew in the 1100s, it was in a continual state of construction and remodeling. At its peak, the whole community—town and surrounding hamlets—may have reached a population of 1,800 people and covered an area of one square mile. The part of the site that is presently a public monument reflects an influence from Chaco Canyon (see p. 119), the center of an Anasazi subculture to the south. Lowry is believed to be the northernmost Chacoan outlier. Chacoans also lived at nearby Escalante Pueblo (see p. 46), and their influence is seen elsewhere in the Northern San Juan region.

Visitors to Lowry will see a cluster of rooms with one-story standing walls admirably constructed of neatly cut stones in the Chacoan masonry tradition. A great kiva near the pueblo dating to about A.D. 1085 also has been excavated and stabilized for viewing. This would have been a gathering point for the entire community. One interesting feature is the painted kiva located in one of the room blocks. Built around 1103, its walls were decorated with designs painted on plaster. The kiva has been roofed to protect its paintings; still, they have proven to be very vulnerable to moisture damage and temperature changes since being exposed to the air. Lowry is thought to have been abandoned soon after A.D. 1200. New excavations at the site in the early 1990s by Fort Lewis College and Colorado State University students should throw more light on the history of this pueblo community.

Lowry Pueblo Ruins were missed by the 1776 Dominguez-Escalante Expedition and missed also by the Hayden Expedition of 1881. Subsequent settlers gave the site little notice, and it was not recorded until 1919. It was named for George Lowry, an early homesteader, and was first excavated in the 1930s by Paul S. Martin of the Chicago Field Museum of Natural History. The Bureau of Land Management administers the site today.

As you approach Lowry, you will notice the mounds of an unexcavated pueblo off the road on the left. Lowry is only a short distance farther. There are picnic tables near the site, and

Lowry Pueblo Ruins.

brochures are available to guide you along the ruins trail. The site is open daily.

The town of Cortez is a center for travel services. Other nearby ruins include Hovenweep National Monument (see p. 51), the Escalante and Dominguez ruins (see p. 46), Sand Canyon Pueblo (see p. 49), and Mesa Verde National Park (see p. 36).

Suggested reading: *Lowry Ruin in Southwestern Colorado,* by Paul S. Martin et al., Field Museum of Natural History Publication 356, Anthropological Series 23(1), Chicago, Illinois, 1936.

Three Kiva Pueblo

Three Kiva Pueblo is located in Montezuma Canyon, in southeastern Utah. The site is along the Montezuma Canyon Road about 15 miles north of Hatch Trading Post and 23 miles south of the road's intersection with U.S. 163, south of Monticello. From Blanding, Utah, a gravel road leads east to the Montezuma Canyon Road at a point about 6 miles south of the site. For current information on road conditions in this area, call the Bureau of Land Management at (801) 587-2141.

Three Kiva Pueblo, a fourteen-room Anasazi site, is an out-of-the-way Indian ruin that will probably be of more interest to archaeology buffs than casual tourists. Montezuma Canyon is an arid, unpopulated stretch of country, the scenic charm of which lies in contrasts between spare, rugged mesas and cottonwood-shaded dry washes. Much of this territory belongs to the Ute and Navajo tribes, the successors to the Anasazi Indians who lived here 700 to 1,000 years ago.

Before describing the site itself, it is only fair to mention that the drive involves a typical desert-country road that crisscrosses a dry wash at numerous junctions. Under normal conditions, this presents no difficulty; however, flash floods do occur, and flooding can deposit wide expanses of deep sand capable of bogging down even four-wheel-drive vehicles.

William Henry Jackson, the noted American photographer and explorer, made the first archaeological reconnaissance of Montezuma Canyon in 1886. Excavations on nearby Alkali Ridge were carried out in 1908 and again in the 1930s. Three Kiva Pueblo itself was excavated between 1969 and 1972 by the Brigham Young University Field School of Archaeology.

The very first section of the site was built in the ninth century. The pueblo subsequently experienced three occupations and building phases with its main occupation between A.D. 1000 and

Three Kiva Pueblo.

1300. Its earliest occupants were of the Kayenta branch of the Anasazi, whose central territory lay some distance to the south. But later, the Three Kiva people maintained closer ties with their Mesa Verde and Hovenweep neighbors to the east.

The pueblo was laid out as a square. Windblown fill on a kiva floor under the collapsed roof measured over two feet in depth—a clue that the kiva survived intact for a long time after the people left. Just south of the pueblo is an interesting two-by-twenty foot masonry room identified as a turkey run from the abundance of excavated turkey bones. Domesticated turkeys were an important source of food to the Anasazi, not just here but at many other sites. In addition to eating turkeys, the Indians wove feather blankets and made whistles from their leg bones.

In the course of the site's excavations, diggers found two abalone shell pendants, evidence that a trade network existed to the Pacific Coast. Predictably, they also found many stone tools: knives, scrapers, drills, spear and arrow points, hammer stones, hoes, axes, mauls, dishes, manos, and metates. Findings such as these help archaeologists reconstruct a picture of daily life at the pueblo hundreds of years ago.

The Bureau of Land Management manages the Three Kiva Pueblo site and has restored one of the kivas, which visitors are welcome to enter by ladder. Also, enterprising rock art hunters will find petroglyphs along the east-facing canyon walls down canyon from the site. The glyphs include buffalos, cranes, and other animal and abstract figures.

Although travelers to Three Kiva Pueblo should watch road conditions, the site is worth seeing, especially for those with a special interest in the prehistory of this area. Gas, restaurants, and overnight accommodations can be found in Bluff, Blanding, and Monticello.

> Suggested reading: "A Synthesis of Excavations at Site 42SA863, Three Kiva Pueblo, Montezuma Canyon, San Juan County, Utah," by Donald E. Miller, 1974, Master's thesis, available through Brigham Young University, Provo, Utah.

Edge of the Cedars State Park

Edge of the Cedars State Park is in the southeastern Utah town of Blanding on U.S. 163 between Bluff and Monticello. Directions to the park are clearly marked in town.

Edge of the Cedars Pueblo is a medium-sized ruin on the northern periphery of Anasazi territory. The site, which sits on a ridge overlooking Westwater Canyon, has a panoramic view of many miles of countryside. To the north lie the Abajo ("Blue") Mountains, an important prehistoric area for hunting and foraging, and to the southeast you can see the famous landmark of Shiprock in New Mexico. In ancient times, this well-watered region was a veritable "breadbasket" that supported a high-density aboriginal population. Old timers in Blanding have reported seeing the remnants of irrigation ditches and check dams around the Edge of the Cedars Pueblo.

The pueblo was certainly occupied between A.D. 850 and 950 and again between 1025 and 1125. Some tree-ring dates point to a thirteenth-century occupation as well but this is unsubstantiated by ceramic evidence. The site consists of six residential complexes, about ten kivas, and one great kiva. The great kiva, which probably functioned as a community center, remains unexcavated and appears as a large shallow basin in the ground. Another kiva, however, has been excavated and restored and may be entered by means of a ladder that descends a hatchway in the roof. A small room block has been restored as well. The original village probably extended beyond its present park boundaries before early settlers cultivated the land to grow crops, in the process obliterating archaeological traces.

Weber State College field school excavated about 25 percent

Edge of the Cedars Pueblo.

of the pueblo between 1969 and 1972. The outcome of these investigations was disappointing because of apparent lax student supervision, poor documentation, loss of field notes and photographs, and the absence of any final report. Weber State College archaeologists came up with one rather rare find at Edge of the Cedars, a prehistoric copper bell. This tangible object is proof that the northern Anasazi had trading contacts with the high cultures of Mexico, far to the south.

Edge of the Cedars Museum, which is open daily during normal business hours, contains exhibits relating to the various peoples and cultures of southeastern Utah: the Anasazi, Navajo, and Ute Indians, and Anglo-American settlers. It also has an outstanding collection of Anasazi ceramics on exhibit, and some of its walls are decorated with fine large-scale reproductions of pictographs. The museum's trail guide helps visitors understand the site as they walk around the ruins.

Blanding is a small, quiet town with a couple of cafes, gas stations, and motels. This Four Corners region is full of ancient ruins, including many that are open to the public; you can spend days enjoying not only the sites but also the walks and hikes leading to them. Recommended sites near Blanding include Mule Canyon and Cave Tower ruins (see p. 72) and Grand Gulch (see p. 75).

Westwater Ruin

The Westwater Ruin is near Blanding, Utah. Follow U.S. 191 south from Blanding for just over a mile; turn right on County Road 232 and continue 2 miles to the ruins overlook.

Just south of Blanding, Utah, an Anasazi cliff dwelling sits tucked in a large rock alcove along the west wall of Westwater Canyon. Lush undergrowth on the canyon floor engulfs a small, flowing creek, hinting at the desirability of the site to prehistoric farmers. The canyon has other ruins including the much larger Edge of the Cedars Pueblo (see p. 60) upstream.

A tree-ring core taken in 1936 from a Westwater roof beam revealed a cutting date of A.D. 1243, but the site is believed to have been occupied as early as A.D. 750. Its occupants were culturally affiliated with the Mesa Verde Anasazi to the southeast. Westwater Pueblo consisted of thirteen ground-level rooms, five kivas, and some now collapsed upper-story rooms. These habitations were divided into two main room blocks under the cliff.

Westwater is one of so many archaeological sites throughout the Southwest that have been damaged by pothunters, vandals, and careless visitors. Walls have been pushed over and holes dug in the floor fill. What remains are a few knee- and waist-high structures.

From the roadside overlook, visitors have a good view of the site. A short steep trail also leads down to the ruins. The poor condition of this cliff dwelling, however, and the absence of interpretation at the site will disappoint many people who choose to make the walk across the canyon.

Newspaper Rock

Newspaper Rock, a State Historic Monument in southeastern Utah, is located on the north side of Utah 211, 12 miles west of its intersection with U.S. 163, north of Monticello.

There are numerous so-called newspaper rocks in the West. One of the finest examples is Newspaper Rock, near Canyonlands in southeastern Utah. Here, etched in the dark patina of a single smooth rock slab, are literally hundreds of figures from a number of Native American cultures—Archaic, Basketmaker, Fremont, Anasazi, Ute, Navajo—as well as Spanish- and Anglo-American. The petroglyphs are protected from the elements by a natural overhang that seems to have been custom-made for the purpose. In addition, the panel sits behind a security railing,

Newspaper Rock.

which helps safeguard it from contemporary vandalism.

Dating presents a major, though not totally insurmountable, challenge to students of Indian rock art. A reliable time frame can often be determined when a petroglyph or pictograph site is clearly associated with other cultural material of a known date, such as a pueblo or cliff dwelling. This is not the case with Newspaper Rock, with which other dating methods must be employed. Observers will note, for example, the presence of several horses and riders. Horses were introduced to the Southwest in 1540 by Spanish conquistadores, but they probably were not owned by natives of this region until after 1680 when the Pueblo Indians drove the Spaniards into exile in Mexico and appropriated their livestock. In this case, historical knowledge helps date a petroglyph.

Scholars, who have assigned rough time periods to certain rock art styles, believe some of the Newspaper Rock pictures go back to the Archaic period, at least 4,000 years ago. Other glyphs here can be attached to certain Indian tribes whose presence in the area is known archaeologically or historically. Rock art students, therefore, in collaboration with other researchers, are slowly building up a body of knowledge about the ancient glyphs that are found in so many locations. But while this academic process continues, the pictures themselves can be appreciated on their own merits by just about anyone. Some images are clear in meaning, some obscure; some are carefully executed, others scrawled in a sloppy fashion; some tell a story, others are abstract. While Newspaper Rock may not have been a newspaper, it nevertheless contains much to read. You can stay here for five minutes or an hour.

Another large panel—Shay Canyon Petroglyphs—may be visited near Newspaper Rock. It contains many anthropomorphic figures as well as depictions of mountain sheep, birds, and abstract designs. To reach this site, continue on Route 211 to an informal pull-off exactly two miles west of Newspaper Rock. Here a rough trail leads down the road embankment, crosses a streambed and flat area, and climbs up a short talus slope to some darkly patinated cliffs where the glyphs are clearly visible. The walk is about 300 yards from the road.

Suggested reading: *Indian Rock Art of the Southwest,* by Polly Schaafsma, University of New Mexico Press, Albuquerque, New Mexico, 1980.

Canyonlands National Park

Canyonlands National Park is located in southeastern Utah. Roads lead into the park from Utah 211, north of Monticello, and from Utah 313, north of Moab. The only other accesses to the park are by jeep trails.

Like the Grand Canyon, Canyonlands is a large park that was set aside for its unique scenic and geologic character. Here eons of erosion have created wondrous landforms: red rock cliffs, pinnacles, and spires; fossil sand dunes; and steep-walled canyons. Within the park, the waters of the Colorado and Green rivers meet to flow through Cataract Canyon, a white-water thriller, and continue on to Lake Powell and the Grand Canyon.

But Canyonlands was also once the home of prehistoric Native Americans who left their mark in the form of small scattered pueblos and granaries and some of the most outstanding galleries of rock art found on the North American continent. Although the national park was established with more thought given to geology than to cultural heritage, many visitors will enjoy bring-

Canyonlands from the Maze Overlook.

ing a prehistorical perspective to their explorations of the area's jeep and hiking trails. This guidebook will offer some general remarks on Canyonlands' human past; visitors wishing to find specific sites should consult park service rangers and obtain a large-scale map.

Archaeologists have done little work within Canyonlands National Park, and much research must still be accomplished before anyone will be able to speak with confidence about the exact sequence of cultures here. At least two prehistoric groups, however, lived in the Canyonlands area. Archaic people, whose culture has been dated to as long ago as 7000 B.C. up to about A.D. 500, left campsites, scatters of stone artifacts, and rock art behind them. While the above dates represent the Archaic period, it is interesting to note that some Archaic traditions survived much longer, as evidenced by the presence of seminomadic hunters and gatherers in parts of the Southwest well into the nineteenth century.

Anasazi sites are found in Canyonlands as well, most dating from about A.D. 950 to 1250. The Anasazi, like their Archaic predecessors, hunted game and gathered many wild plant foods. But their subsistence was more dependent upon agriculture, and the remains of their settlements are found near arable land and sources of water. In Canyonlands, areas suitable for growing crops were limited in size, and water was undependable. Therefore, the Anasazi never concentrated in large pueblos, and their habitations tended to be small and dispersed. When drought struck the Four Corners region in the thirteenth century, this marginal area was one of the first to be abandoned.

A very accessible ruin in the park is Roadside Ruin in the Needles District just off the paved road west of the information center. This site, the condition of which is so pristine as to make the appellation "ruin" a misnomer, is a masonry storage bin built in a small rock shelter. The turn-off to this site is well marked.

Particularly rich archaeological areas in the Needles District of Canyonlands are Salt Canyon and Ruin Park. On the west side of the Green River, fine pictograph panels can be found in the Maze and in Horseshoe Canyon.

Rock art is the most impressive feature left behind by the prehistoric occupants of Canyonlands. Horseshoe Canyon, sometimes called Barrier Canyon, contains exceptional panels of tall, floating, ghost-like figures, believed to date to the late Archaic period. Here, at the Great Gallery, can be found one of the finest series of pictographs in the Barrier Canyon Anthropomorphic Style, which rock art scholar Polly Schaafsma tentatively dates between 500 B.C. and A.D. 500. The artists, who may have been shamans, used a variety of painting techniques to gain special effects.

Barrier Canyon pictographs, Canyonlands National Park.

Sometimes they prepared the rock surface to create a smooth surface. They applied paint directly with their fingers or with yucca brushes, blew pigments through reed tubes, and incised lines through painted areas to achieve texture. Most pigment is dark reddish, often faded, but some figures are decorated with white lines.

Another panel of shamanic figures is located at the Bird Site in the Maze, a relatively inaccessible sector of the park. Here, paintings of supernaturals, some with vertical stripes on their bodies and antennae coming out of their heads, appear to be involved in a harvest scene. They are surrounded by small animals and birds.

Canyonlands has long been considered a frontier zone between the Fremont and Anasazi cultures, and no one is certain which group may have been responsible for some of the rock art. An example is the well-known All American Man site in upper Salt

Creek. Other pictographs in the Faces Motif Anthropomorphic Style can be found throughout the Needles District of the park.

The rock art of Canyonlands is one of this country's most precious aboriginal treasures; hopefully, everyone making the effort to see these sites will treat them with care and respect. In this way, future generations will be able to to appreciate them.

Canyonlands National Park has information centers and camping areas. Persons planning to hike or travel by jeep into the park's backcountry need to be well prepared and supplied. Water is a particular necessity, especially in summer. The nearest towns with travel services are Moab and Monticello. Moab is a regional tourist center with numerous outfitters and tour companies offering raft, jeep, and bicycle trips. For more information, call the Moab Chamber of Commerce.

Suggested reading: *Cultural Resource Inventory and Testing in the Salt Creek Pocket and Devils Lane Areas, Needles District, Canyonlands National Park, Utah,* by Betsy L. Tipps and Nancy J. Hewitt, National Park Service, Denver, Colorado, 1989.

Potash Road Petroglyphs

The Potash Road Petroglyphs are located along the north side of Utah 279, 9 miles west of Moab, Utah. Follow Utah 191 (Potash Road) for 4 miles north of Moab, turn west on 279, and continue 5.5 miles. Here, highway signs mark the petroglyphs, which are visible from your car window and continue for about a mile.

The Potash Road Petroglyphs, located along the north bank of the Colorado River, is an outstanding Indian rock art site. Unlike so much rock art, which is located in remote areas, these panels are readily accessible to anyone wishing to see "Indian writings," as they are often called in Utah, with minimal expenditure of time and effort.

The Potash Road petroglyphs derive from the Fremont culture, remains of which are found today in southern and eastern Utah. The Southern San Raphael Fremont Indians lived on the northern periphery of the Colorado Plateau—thus north of the Anasazi—between roughly A.D. 500 and 1300. These dates are less certain than those of their Anasazi neighbors because of the absence of wood that can be dated in Fremont sites. This group and other Fremont groups to the west and north subsisted by hunting mountain sheep, deer, bison, and other game; gathering wild plant foods; and cultivating corn, beans, and squash. But the Fremont are best known today for the fine examples of rock art

Rock art along Potash Road.

they left behind. Other examples can be found at Newspaper Rock and Shay Canyon (see p. 64), and in the vicinity of Capitol Reef to the west and Dinosaur National Monument to the north.

Along Route 279, you will find many examples of human figures, which are characteristically drawn with broad-shouldered triangular torsos, horns on the heads, and holding spears and shields. Some scenes show lines of people holding hands—probably dancers performing religious ceremonies. Plenty of game animals, such as mountain sheep and deer, and geometrics are also pictured. In addition, you can find horsemen; these figures are probably the work of Ute Indians who lived in the region in later times.

The drive along Route 279 has another reward—the beautiful landscape along the Colorado River. Dramatic sandstone cliffs topped by dunelike bluffs form a dramatic backdrop to the river. From Moab, the Colorado flows south to be joined by the Green

River and continues through Canyonlands National Park, Cataract Canyon, and into Lake Powell. Both the Colorado and Green are favorite rivers for rafters.

From Moab, which is a center for people interested in backcountry hiking, mountain biking, jeeping, and river rafting, you can make a round-trip to see the Potash Road Petroglyphs in one to two hours.

> Suggested reading: *Petroglyphs and Pictographs of Utah*, vol. 2, by Kenneth B. Castleton, Utah Museum of Natural History, Salt Lake City, Utah, 1979.

Butler Wash Ruins

The Butler Wash Ruins in southeastern Utah are along Utah 95, 10.7 miles west of its intersection with Utah 191. The turnoff is clearly marked along the highway. A 1-mile loop trail leads from the parking area to a ruins overlook.

Travelers along Utah 95 will enjoy a driving break to see a lovely cliff dwelling at the head of Butler Wash. From the highway rest area, a fifteen-minute walk leads over the slickrock to a good viewpoint overlooking the site: a well-preserved Anasazi cliff dwelling dating to the A.D. 1200s. In addition to living and storage rooms, the main dwelling contained four kivas.

The pueblo sits on a ledge within a cave in the cliff. Beneath the ledge a second deep overhang provided the inhabitants with great security from potential enemies. The only access to the cliff dwelling was by means of a treacherous hand- and toe-hold trail chipped into the sandstone cliff to the left of the caves. This trail is still clearly visible from the overlook as it winds down the steep rock. However, erosion has obliterated many of the steps. The site's defensibility, which is typical of Anasazi sites in the Four Corners region of the late thirteenth century, suggests that its residents may have lived in fear of attack. However, no actual proof of warfare has yet been found.

Like most cliff dwellings, this one faces south, an orientation that would have provided passive solar heating benefits to its residents in cold weather. In winter, the sun lies low in the sky, and its warming rays penetrate deep within the cave. In summer, on the other hand, the pueblo is shaded by the cliff overhang, thus remaining relatively cool.

Viewers will notice water stains flowing over the cliff edge

Butler Wash cliff dwelling.

directly above the site, evidence of runoff from rains and snow-melt. This convenient drainage facilitated water collection for the pueblo residents, who enjoyed a natural plumbing system. The runoff flowed down canyon where the Butler Wash inhabitants could have directed it to garden plots in which they raised corn, beans, and squash. They stored these products in small masonry storage rooms tucked up under rock ledges. One of these granaries is visible from the overlook to the left of the main cliff dwelling.

Along the trail from the parking area to the site, you will pass numerous desert plants that were useful in one way or another to the Indians. Prickly pear, for example, provides a succulent fruit, and the piñon pine produces edible nuts. The Anasazi also used fibers from the yucca plant to make sandals, baskets, rope, and cloth, and they shredded cliff rose bark to fashion mats and other fabrics. Even juniper berries, which we use to flavor gin, were used as a food seasoning.

Butler Wash flows along the east side of Comb Ridge, a ninety-mile, east-sloping hogback along which many Anasazi sites can be found. This geologic feature, through which Utah 95 makes a dramatic cut just west of Butler Wash, was formed about seventy million years ago.

Other nearby ruins can be found at Mule Canyon (see below), Grand Gulch (see p. 75), and Natural Bridges National Monument (see p. 79). The nearest travel services are in Blanding and Bluff along Utah 191 to the east.

Mule Canyon and Cave Tower Ruins

Mule Canyon Indian Ruins are located along Utah 95, 16 miles east of Natural Bridges National Monument and 20 miles west of the intersection of Utah 95 with U.S. 191. The turnoff to Cave Tower Ruins is .7 miles east of the Mule Canyon exit. To reach the ruins, drive .7 miles on this backroad and park. The ruins are about a 5-minute walk farther.

Mule Canyon Indian Ruins are located in southeastern Utah about twenty-five miles north of the San Juan River. The pueblo was inhabited in the eleventh and twelfth centuries when Anasazi culture was at its height in the Four Corners region and penetrated deep into southern Utah.

Mule Canyon Pueblo consisted of an *L*-shaped room block with twelve masonry rooms that probably was the home of two extended families. In addition, there were two kivas and a two-story tower. The room block was used for living, storing food and supplies, and as a work area in bad weather. Most daily activities,

Kiva at Mule Canyon Ruins.

however, took place on the rooftops and in the plaza in front of the pueblo. The surrounding area offered possibilities for hunting game, gathering wild plants and seeds, and farming.

For a small site, Mule Canyon holds several interesting features. The tower, for example, may have been part of a communications network linking this pueblo with others in the vicinity; it has a direct line of sight to Cave Towers, a mile to the east. An unusual tunnel connects the tower to the kiva and a second tunnel connects the kiva to the room block. Whether the tunnels to the kiva had a practical function or were used in rituals is an open question. The kiva also had a rooftop entrance by means of a ladder descending a hatchway. Other kiva features include a wall niche, "foot drum," pilasters to support roof beams, firepit, stone deflector, and ventilator shaft to draw in fresh air.

Mule Canyon Pueblo was first occupied about A.D. 750 and had a major occupation between 1000 and 1150. The style of pottery and architecture at the site suggest that people from both the Mesa Verde area to the east and the Kayenta area to the south lived here. The site was excavated by the University of Utah and developed by the Bureau of Land Management in connection with the construction of Utah 95 in the early 1970s. The building of this highway was a major project, funded with bicentennial

Cave Tower Ruins.

grants, opening up a large wilderness area that had previously been inaccessible to large numbers of people. The project generated controversy between developers and conservationists and inspired a popular novel, *The Monkey Wrench Gang*, by the late Edward Abbey.

Nearby Cave Towers consists of half a dozen towers and several cliff dwellings. Individuals with a strong interest in the Anasazi will enjoy exploring these undeveloped ruins. The unexcavated, unstabilized towers are clustered on the mesa around the head of Mule Canyon and probably housed small families. Dividing the community is an intermittent stream, which was probably dammed up to create a small reservoir. The stream flows over the upper rim of the canyon and forms a substantial pool beneath, which the residents must have enjoyed in hot weather.

The cliff dwellings are a challenge to reach. For a good view of them, walk along the west rim of the canyon beyond the towers and look across the canyon. Binoculars will help. Visitors with an exploratory bent can find a rough trail on the east side of the canyon rim that leads down to the cliff house level. Anyone visiting Cave Towers should remember that because of their instability, the ruins should not be climbed on or disturbed, and any potsherds or other artifacts should be left in place. These seemingly trivial bits and pieces from antiquity may one day help tell the story of the Anasazi of this region.

Other nearby ruins can be found at Butler Wash (see p. 70), Grand Gulch (below), and Natural Bridges National Monument (see p. 79). Bluff and Blanding have food, gas, and other travel services.

Grand Gulch Primitive Area

Grand Gulch is a tributary of the San Juan River in southeastern Utah. Permits to enter the gulch may be obtained at the Bureau of Land Management's Kane Gulch Ranger Station on Utah 261, 6 miles south of this highway's intersection with Utah 95. For further information, call (801) 587-2141.

Grand Gulch is a long narrow canyon in southeastern Utah that meanders some sixty miles southwards across Cedar Mesa to the San Juan River. Its intermittent creek, fed by snow melt, seasonal rains, and occasional springs, provides water for lush undergrowth along the canyon floor from which sheer cliffs rise to the surrounding tableland. Grand Gulch was long inhabited by the Anasazi, whose cliff houses and granaries remain neatly tucked into rock shelters and crannies. The canyon walls also contain many fine panels of pictographs and petroglyphs.

Round House, Grand Gulch Primitive Area.

Grand Gulch lies far off the beaten tourist track and is accessible only to hikers, backpackers, and horseback riders. To visit the area requires considerable time, planning, and physical activity. However, it is a beautiful and archaeologically rich area that holds much reward for anyone willing to make the effort to walk through it.

Numerous amateur and professional archaeologists have worked in Grand Gulch over the past century. Their surveys and excavations, while resulting in large artifact collections, have contributed little to our knowledge of southwestern prehistory. In 1893–1894 and 1896–1897, Richard Wetherill of Mesa Verde fame conducted major collecting expeditions through the gulch, and the vast quantities of material he extracted from the ruins presently lie in the vaults of the American Museum of Natural History in New York and the Chicago Field Museum. In more recent years, research in Grand Gulch and on Cedar Mesa has been done by William D. Lipe and others; however, little has been published on the canyon's prehistory beyond esoteric papers in specialized journals.

If Grand Gulch's archaeological record leaves something to be desired, the canyon itself remains an extraordinary outdoor Anasazi museum. Its first permanent residents were Basketmaker people who had camps in rock shelters as early as A.D. 200 to 400. They depended mostly on hunting and gathering but also prac-ticed a degree of horticulture in the canyon. Interestingly, when Wetherill excavated these preceramic Basketmaker II sites in Grand Gulch, he recognized that they represented a distinct culture antedating the Pueblo remains that overlay them. His theory of an earlier "basket people," which was later verified by trained archaeologists, was an uncredited breakthrough in the understanding of southwestern prehistory. After A.D. 500, the Basketmakers invented pottery, lived in pithouses, and practiced agriculture on a full-time basis.

Little evidence has been found that the Anasazi were living in Grand Gulch between A.D. 700 and 1000, but from then until the late 1200s, they flourished here. By 1300, however, they had gone for good, leaving behind them a multitude of cliff houses, many of which remain well preserved. In some cases, pristine roofs and ceilings cover standing masonry walls whose mud plaster still retains the fingerprints of its Anasazi makers.

Grand Gulch's unique charm is that you can experience its antiquities on your own and in relative solitude. This privilege carries with it a measure of responsibility both to yourself and to the ruins. It is important to anyone entering the area to bring sufficient food and water and to take care to avoid hiking accidents. It is also essential to treat the cliff houses and rock art panels with respect and not to climb on walls or collect artifacts. At many sites, visitors have placed a variety of items such as potsherds, stone flakes, and dried corn cobs on flat rocks for others to view; their presence adds to the excitement of seeing the ruins.

After outfitting for a trip into the gulch, you should register at the Kane Gulch Ranger Station and obtain a hiking map of the area. Rangers will provide information on the locations of Junction Ruin, Turkey Pen Ruin, Round House, Banister Ruins, the Green Mask Site, the F.B.I. Panel, the Big Man Panel, and other sites. Turkey Pen Ruin, which had an 1,100-year span of occupations, was first excavated by Richard Wetherill, who complained about the difficulty of digging through deep layers of desiccated turkey dung. Until 1979, this site offered the best potential for future research of any ruins in the gulch. In the fall of that year, looters ransacked the ruins in search of marketable antiquities and even burned ancient roof beams to keep warm as they dug their holes through the night.

There are several ways to visit Grand Gulch depending on your available time and budget. A two- or three-day visit may be accomplished by backpacking in and out of the canyon by way of Kane Gulch, Bullit Canyon, or Collins Spring. Alternately, you could enter by way of Kane Gulch, hike down canyon, exit by way of Bullit, then walk or hitchhike back to the starting point. A luxurious way to experience the gulch is with a profes-

Pictographs in Grand Gulch.

sional outfitter to carry food and gear on horseback and prepare meals. An outfitter can be found in Moab. Perhaps the ultimate experience, however, is to float down the San Juan River (see p. 82) by raft from Bluff to the mouth of Grand Gulch, be met there by an outfitter with horses, and ride up to Bullit or Kane Gulch. This would be about a ten-day trip.

Grand Gulch offers no accommodations or travel services and is closed to vehicles. Drinking water is only seasonally available at a few springs. Spring and fall are the best times to hike here as temperatures can be very hot in summer and frigid in winter. Backpacking trips in the gulch are best suited for people experienced in hiking and camping in the backcountry.

> Suggested reading: *Grand Gulch Primitive Area,* a brochure and hiking map published by the Bureau of Land Management, P.O. Box 970, Moab, Utah 84532.

Natural Bridges National Monument

Natural Bridges National Monument is located along Interstate 95, 26 miles east of Fry Canyon and 42 miles west of Blanding, Utah.

In 1908, President Theodore Roosevelt set aside over 7,000 acres of land around upper White Canyon, Utah, to safeguard three beautiful geologic formations called "bridges." The park area, however, had long ago been a haven of the Anasazi Indians and contains sites where they lived.

The natural bridges of White Canyon were first recorded at the late date of 1883, for this is a rugged region that was little penetrated by explorers and pioneers until recent times and is still largely unsettled. Archaeologists completed the first major survey of the upper canyon in 1961, reporting 200 archaeological sites spanning about thirteen centuries of Anasazi occupation. Many sites were small, collapsed, or buried structures on the juniper- and sage-covered mesa, but the surveyors also found pueblos, kivas, granaries, and rock art within the canyon.

Some cliff dwellings have survived in remarkably fine condition—even with roofs intact—a clue that they had been abruptly and peaceably abandoned and never again reoccupied. When Pueblo Indians moved, they often carried their valuable roof timbers with them for reuse in their next home because large trees were hard to fell with stone axes. Another factor contributing to the fine preservation of these sites was that, in later times, neither Navajos, Utes, nor European-Americans made their homes here. Indeed, for 600 years, these habitations were left undisturbed.

Regular use of White Canyon may have begun as early as 2,000 years ago. Certainly from about A.D. 450, the canyon witnessed a stable population; in the mid-1100s, however, there was an influx of people and a spurt of building. All indications are that these people were Mesa Verdean in their culture but also carried on trade with the Kayenta Anasazi, who lived to the south. One interesting phenomenon that archaeologists have noted here and elsewhere is a cultural lag between what was happening in the Anasazi heartland along the San Juan River and developments on the northern periphery of their world. This is noticeable in the archaeological record in pottery designs and building styles.

The latest tree-ring date at Natural Bridges—the last year when a tree was cut to build a house—was A.D. 1251. A building slump usually signals a population decline, and this is the same period when the Anasazi world as a whole was beginning to change. The residents of White Canyon were not spared whatever economic hardships or social disruptions were being experienced by other communities in the Four Corners region.

Anasazi handprints at Kachina Bridge, Natural Bridges National Monument.

An eight-mile driving loop leads to scenic overlooks at Sipapu, Kachina, and Owachomo Bridges. Natural Bridges focuses on its natural rather than cultural history; consequently, the park service offers only minimal interpretation of its human prehistory. Nevertheless, visitors can visit a number of ancient sites by hiking through White Canyon.

Rangers at the visitor center will help you find specific ruins and will no doubt caution you about their extreme fragility. Inner-canyon hiking is easy but the switchback trails in and out are strenuous, especially in hot weather. The main trail through the canyon begins along the roadside at Sipapu Bridge and leads to Kachina Bridge. A short distance down this trail, on the right hand side, just downstream from Deer Canyon, you can view Horsecollar Ruins. At Kachina Bridge, there are several mud huts under a broad rock overhang on which a number of petroglyphs and pictographs are visible. One of these is a well-preserved row of painted handprints, a popular Anasazi motif. Most of the rock art in White Canyon dates from A.D. 950 to 1300.

The Natural Bridges visitor center has interpretive exhibits and a slide program on the area's geology. The monument also has a small campground but no food, gas, or camping supplies can be purchased here. The nearest places to obtain these are at Fry Canyon, Blanding, and Mexican Hat. Grand Gulch (see p. 75) is only a few miles south on Highway 261, and Mule Canyon Ruins (see p. 72) are about sixteen miles east on the way to Blanding.

Suggested reading: *An Archaeological Survey of the Upper White Canyon Area, Southeastern Utah,* by Philip M. and Audrey E. Hobler, Utah State Historical Society, Salt Lake City, Utah, 1978.

Anasazi State Park

Anasazi State Park is located in the town of Boulder, Utah, which is along Utah 12 in the south-central part of the state.

When Kayenta Anasazi people established a village about A.D. 1075 off the southern edge of the Aquarius Plateau in what is now southern Utah, they had every reason to anticipate a prosperous existence. The area had fertile soils; reliable streams; plentiful game; abundant firewood; and materials for house building and the manufacture of pottery, tools, utensils, and clothing. Even the climate favored them—pleasant in summer, not too harsh in winter. Compared with settlements in the Grand Canyon to the south, life at this Kayenta outpost was relatively easy.

Once established, the occupants of this village carried on farming along the streams and in irrigated fields, hunted game ranging from bighorn sheep and mule deer to rabbits, and gathered many wild edible plants and seeds. Although they brought with them customs and traits from their Kayenta region of origin, they soon were influenced by local Fremont people and other Anasazi groups. Archaeologists believe the village, known as the Coombs site, functioned as a cultural crossroads between Kayenta populations to the south and neighboring groups of central and western Utah. Certainly it is one of the westernmost communities of the Anasazi, whose heartland lay in the Four Corners region far to the east.

The Coombs village thrived until about A.D. 1275 when it was almost completely destroyed by fire. What caused the conflagration is impossible to determine today but accidental fires were a common problem in pueblos and were hard to control once started. The main cause of fires, presumably, was that sparks from small cooking and heating fires within the room blocks would ignite dry grass or twigs used as construction materials in the ceilings.

Another mystery is where the Coombs people went after the disaster. As yet, no sites have been excavated that show a later occupation by these folk. Perhaps they broke up into small groups and returned south and east to join other Anasazi communities along the San Juan River. Their village, soon to be covered by dust and blowing sand, lay undisturbed for seven centuries.

The Coombs site was excavated in the 1950s as part of an extensive archaeological salvage project resulting from the building of Glen Canyon Dam. Although the waters of Lake Powell lie forty-five miles distant, research at this site, one of the largest Anasazi ruins west of the Colorado River, was deemed essential to better understand the prehistory of the inundated region, which itself had few village sites.

Coombs Village, ca. A.D. 1100, at Anasazi State Park.
Courtesy University of Utah Press. Restoration by George A. King.

The Coombs village is part of Anasazi State Park, which includes a visitor center, museum, and picnic area. The park is open daily on a year-round basis. The nearest travel services are in Escalante, the next town south on Utah 12.

> Suggested reading: *The Coombs Site*, 3 vols., by Robert H. Lister, University of Utah Press, Salt Lake City, Utah, 1959-1961.

San Juan River

The San Juan River rises in the mountains of south-central Colorado, dips down into northwestern New Mexico, bends north to flow past the Four Corners area into southeastern Utah, and continues west to Lake Powell, where its waters mingle with those of the Colorado River.

As the principal drainage of the Colorado Plateau, the San Juan River and its tributaries were the cradle of Anasazi culture. The Anasazi, ancestors of the Pueblo Indians of New Mexico and Arizona, depended upon the presence of water for their existence. Most of their religious ceremonies were directed toward attracting rain for crops. Wherever there was water, the Anasazi were likely to be found damming it, digging irrigation ditches, carrying water jugs to their homes, and fishing.

Many Indian ruins can be found along the San Juan River. Some, like Salmon Pueblo (see p. 131), were built upon terraces just above the flood plain. Others, such as Chimney Rock Pueblo, look down on one of the river's major tributaries, the Piedra. But unlike those at Salmon and Chimney Rock, the archaeological sites along the river are not accessable by car. There is a better way to see them—by raft or canoe.

An enterprising rafter or canoeist can float or paddle downstream and discover, not far from the river's banks, the remains of pithouses and pueblos as well as pañels of rock art. The only problem is that you have to know where to look, what to look for, and, upon finding something, understand what it means—not an easy task for the layperson.

A number of river rafting companies operate recreational float trips down the San Juan River, and some, such as Wild Rivers Expeditions in Bluff, Utah, specialize in bringing an educational dimension to the experience. Arrangements can be made to bring along an archaeologist and/or geologist as guide and interpreter. Rafting companies begin trips as far upstream as Montezuma Creek. The rafts float past the towns of Bluff and Mexican Hat to the Goosenecks and ultimately to Lake Powell. This long stretch of river can be broken down to smaller segments; trips, in fact, can vary in length from one to ten or twelve days.

The location of most archaeological sites in this area—whether they are administered by the Bureau of Land Management, the U. S. Forest Service, or the Navajo Nation—is not generally known, a factor which helps to protect them from vandalism, pot hunting, and overuse by river runners. A few sites, however, such as the Sand Island petroglyphs (see p. 85), the Butler Wash petroglyph site, the Moki Steps, and River House, are more widely known and are frequent stops on river trips. Rafting companies also take their clients to other sites and lead hiking excursions up side canyons.

Archaeology aside, rafting the San Juan River is a memorable experience. This usually gentle river runs through lovely pastoral countryside as well as steep-walled canyons with unusual geologic features. Trips include optional walking/hiking side trips to visit geological and archaeological sites. A trip with a focus on the river's Anasazi past will give you a special appreciation of human history and culture in the Four Corners region.

For a set trip fee, rafting companies provide equipment, food, and essential personnel—boat operators, cooks, and guides. All you need do is make a reservation and show up with appropriate personal gear. From then on, weather cooperating, it is pure fun

The Moki Steps along the San Juan River.

punctuated by moments of excitement. A number of nonprofit organizations, such as the Crow Canyon Archaeological Center (800-422-8975), that support research or conservation in the fields of natural history or archaeology also arrange river-rafting trips for their members, supplying their own educational programs. Members receive notices of their scheduled trips.

Travel facilities convenient to San Juan River trips can be found in Bluff and Mexican Hat, Utah. A good starting point for obtaining further information would be to call Wild Rivers Expeditions (800-422-7654) or Recapture Lodge (801-672-2281) in Bluff.

Suggested reading: *The Bright Edge,* by Stephen Trimble, The Museum of Northern Arizona, Flagstaff, Arizona, 1979.

Sand Island Petroglyph Site

The Sand Island Petroglyph Site is located along a cliff bordering the San Juan River two miles west of Bluff, Utah, on U.S. 163. The turn-off to the site is signed from the highway.

The Sand Island petroglyphs look out over the San Juan River in the Anasazi heartland. Grand Gulch lies to the west, Mesa Verde and Hovenweep to the east, Navajo National Monument to the southwest, Chaco Canyon to the southeast, and Edge of the Cedars to the north.

In contrast to rock art sites in Grand Gulch, for example, this extensive petroglyph panel is easily accessible. It includes scores, if not hundreds, of Basketmaker and Pueblo glyphs that range from animals and birds to masks and abstract geometric designs. Also pictured are Kokopellis, the mythic, often-baudy humpbacked fluteplayers familiar in Pueblo graphics from prehistoric to contemporary times. Kokopelli, which is also a Hopi kachina, is lively and virile, a symbol of fertility.

The Sand Island petroglyphs are old, and their dark patina against the patina of the rocks results in a dark-on-dark effect that is hard to photograph, especially in the usual glare of the sun. Also, to protect them from vandalism, a cyclone fence has been constructed in front of the site. The apparent necessity for this fence is unfortunate, since it creates a barrier between viewer (and camera) and the petroglyphs.

Near the petroglyphs is a small, rustic, attractive campground, as well as a popular launching site for river rafters. Bluff, a historic Mormon community, has numerous travel facilities and eating establishments, including Recapture Lodge, the staff of which can direct you to many nearby archaeological and natural

Depiction of Kokopelli, the humpbacked flute player, at Sand Island Petroglyph Site.

history attractions. In addition to ruins, this region contains unsurpassed scenery, such as Monument Valley and Valley of the Gods.

Suggested reading: *Prehistoric Rock Art*, by F. A. Barnes, Wasatch Publishers, Salt Lake City, Utah, 1982.

Navajo National Monument

Navajo National Monument is located in northeastern Arizona. To reach it, follow U.S. 160 northeast 50 miles from Tuba City, Arizona, or southwest 22 miles from Kayenta, Arizona. At this point, a 9-mile paved road leads to the monument. For current information on hiking to ruins, call (602) 672-2366.

Viewed from a distance, Kiet Siel and Betatakin, two magnificent Anasazi cliff dwellings at Navajo National Monument, appear miniature and fragile in relation to the vaulted rock alcoves that shelter them. But they are two of the largest and best preserved cliff houses in the Southwest. Far from major highways, in a remote canyon-cut sector of the Navajo Reservation, they both require some planning and commitment of time and energy to fully appreciate.

The inhabitants of Kiet Siel and Betatakin were Kayenta Anasazi, a third branch of this prehistoric Puebloan people. Like their Mesa Verdean and Chacoan neighbors to the east, the Kayenta were successful farmers, builders, and craftsmen. Artifacts such as ceramics and architecture at Kayenta sites help archaeologists identify them as a distinct branch of the Anasazi that emerged between A.D. 900 and 1100. In the 1100s and 1200s, Kayenta cultural territory extended over the western flank of the San Juan region, reaching west to the Grand Canyon, east to the Chuska Mountains, north into southern Utah, and south to the Hopi Mesas.

Betatakin and Kiet Siel were built in the 1260s and 1270s, occupied for only two or three generations, and abandoned about A.D. 1300. Archaeologists have tried to determine why the Anasazi consolidated into large protected and defensive sites during the latter part of the thirteenth century, then abandoned the region altogether. While Betatakin and Kiet Siel are close to springs, other contemporary pueblos are perched defensively atop almost inaccessible mesas, which would have made daily hikes to water sources and agricultural fields a major inconvenience.

One theory is that formerly productive agricultural lands in the alluvial valleys farther down Tsegi Canyon were damaged in the middle of the century by a shift in weather patterns from winter-dominant precipitation, characterized by gentle rains and snows, to intense summer thunderstorms. Ensuing sheet erosion caused widespread loss of farmland, arroyo cutting, and lower water tables, thereby inhibiting irrigation. These problems were then compounded by drought. Stressed by famine, the scattered Kayenta settlements drew together for protection. The reason for the need for protection is uncertain. Perhaps groups in neighboring canyon systems were raiding each other for food, or possibly attack-

ers came from afar. While this theory that environmental stress spawned warfare has merit, it has yet to be substantiated by evidence of actual fighting. What is certain is that by A.D. 1300, the Anasazi left this area and the Four Corners region in general. Traces of Kayenta-style pottery and architecture have been found in central Arizona, but beyond this, little is known about where they went.

Visitors can view Betatakin from an overlook near the visitor center. Normally, between 1 May and 31 October, the park service conducts a daily morning and afternoon tour to the cliff dwelling, weather permitting. The tour takes about five hours and involves five miles of hiking a steep trail. In 1990, however, the Betatakin tours were canceled for budgetary reasons, so you should call the monument in advance for current information.

Betatakin ruins are strung along a long ledge (betatakin means "ledge house" in Navajo) under the protection of a 500-foot cliff overhang. The tour leads through much of the ruins to view 700 year-old houses with walls and roofs intact. The site looks out over Betatakin Canyon with its stands of scrub oak, pine trees, and lush vegetation. Late summer showers can send a series of thin waterfalls over the cliff from the slickrock mesa above, but not a drop of water touches the ancient Anasazi dwellings.

Betatakin is believed to have been planned and constructed as an entire unit, then occupied by a single group of people. When the ruins were first explored by John Wetherill and Byron Cummings in 1907, they were in excellent condition and contained a large assortment of artifacts. Navajos who lived in the area had long known of this and other cliff dwellings but stayed away, believing the sites were haunted by Anasazi spirits. This no doubt contributed to their fine preservation.

Kiet Siel is located up a tributary of Tsegi Canyon, eight miles from the visitor center. It was "discovered" by Richard Wetherill, the Mancos, Colorado, rancher who earlier had explored the cliff dwellings of Mesa Verde. The site, which contains 155 rooms and 6 kivas, has a view over a lovely valley complete with stream, cottonwood groves, and meadows. Most of the pueblo was built in the 1270s, but its oldest section predates Betatakin by about seventeen years. Due to its fine condition, Kiet Siel gives the feeling of having been abandoned only a couple of generations ago. The roof beams of most rooms are intact, and archaeologists have obtained such precise tree-ring dates as to be able to reconstruct the building sequence of the site room by room.

You can visit Kiet Siel by foot or horseback on a scenic trail that traverses country owned by the Navajo Nation. Horseback excur-

Kiet Siel, Navajo National Monument.

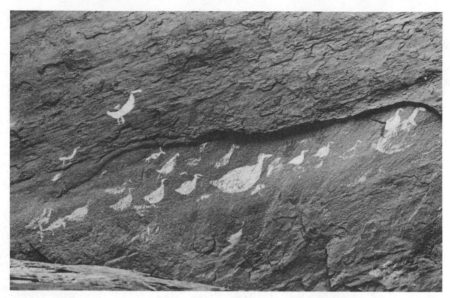

Pictographs in Turkey Cave near Kiet Siel Ruins.

sions with a Navajo guide leave in the morning and return in the afternoon. Reservations and a picnic lunch are needed. Since the hike is long and arduous in places, most people camp overnight at Kiet Siel campground. To do this, you must pack in food, water, and bed rolls. Still another option is to walk to Kiet Siel but arrange to have pack horses carry in camping supplies. Kiet Siel is normally open from Memorial Day to Labor Day and then is limited to twenty people per day. In 1990, again due to budgetary constraints, the site was closed four days a week even in its open season. The site is closed the rest of the year. Reservations to visit Kiet Siel and to rent horses must be made in advance.

Navajo National Monument has a visitor center with an interpretive slide program and small museum display. There also are picnic areas and a small campground. Campfire talks on the area's archaeology, history, and natural history are held in summer. Gas is available along U.S. 160, and restaurants and motels can be found in Kayenta.

Suggested reading: "The Evolution of the Kayenta Anasazi," by Jonathan Haas, in *Canyon de Chelly and Navajo National Monument,* Ancient City Press, Santa Fe, New Mexico, 1986.

Canyon de Chelly National Monument

Canyon de Chelly National Monument is located just off Arizona 63, in Chinle, Arizona. To reach Chinle, drive 65 miles south from U.S. 160, or 33 miles north from U.S. 264. Canyon de Chelly is 95 miles from Gallup, New Mexico.

Viewed from its rim, Canyon de Chelly (pronounced shaye), a thousand feet below, seems like a fertile cradle of life neatly carved through the colorful sandstone formations of northern Arizona's plateau country. A glistening thread of water meanders along the canyon floor past Navajo hogans and sheep pens, orchards, and fields. In spring, the Rio de Chelly, which rises near the Chuska Mountains along the Arizona–New Mexico border, is full, and after summer cloudbursts, it grows to a raging torrent. This canyon is one of the loveliest and most serene places in North America.

Canyon de Chelly (*Chelly* is a Hispanicized version of the Navajo word *Tseyi*, literally meaning "among the rocks" or "canyon") and its tributary Canyon del Muerto have sustained and sheltered human beings for over two millennia. But the history of humans here climaxed between about A.D. 1050 and 1300 when Anasazi Indians lived here in large numbers and built dramatic cliff dwellings, such as White House, Antelope House, Standing Cow Ruins, Sliding Rock Ruins, Junction Ruins, and Mummy Cave. The canyon cliffs also contain a wealth of Anasazi and Navajo petroglyphs and pictographs.

Basketmaker II people, the canyons' first permanent residents, began building pithouses here between A.D. 300 and 420. Sometime after 550, these early occupants learned the craft of pottery-making and began using the bow and arrow. They practiced primitive horticulture, gathered plants and seeds, and hunted game. Their pithouses have been hard to find since they are usually buried beneath the layers of later occupations. One sizable village, Tse Yaa Tsoh, was sheltered in an immense Canyon del Muerto alcove, and excavations at other sites, such as Mummy Cave, Big Cave, and Battle Cove, have given archaeologists a rough picture of Basketmaker life in the canyons.

The presence of water, natural rock shelters, and fertile soils made up an environment that fostered a growing population and allowed Basketmaker settlements to spread up both canyons. During the following Pueblo period (after A.D. 700), the Indians of de Chelly began to live in above-ground masonry houses, produce a variety of crafts, and depend more heavily upon farming within the canyon. Their numbers slowly increased, and they developed a more structured society and elaborate religious life. Some archaeologists, who have extensively surveyed sites in Canyon de Chelly, believe that the modest population of the canyons between A.D. 850 and 1050 may have increased sixfold by 1150. The Anasazi expanded many villages, such as Antelope House and Mummy Cave; commenced construction of new villiages, such as White House, Battle Cove, and Ledge; and built even more villages on the Defiance Plateau outside the canyon.

After A.D. 1150, the Anasazi left their plateau villages to congregate in large cliff dwellings. Why cliff dwellings? This question can spark heated discussions among archaeologists. Some argue that cliff dwellings offered effective defense against a hostile threat, and indeed they would have. Others emphasize the importance of moving off the flood plain to avoid being swept away by floods and to take advantage of precious arable land. Archaeologists also point out that residents of cliff dwellings, which were built under broad alcoves, did not have to rush indoors whenever it rained; the shelters kept their valuable agricultural produce dry; and the shelters faced south, which provided solar warmth in winter.

In the twelfth and thirteenth centuries, Indians from other areas, such as Mesa Verde and perhaps Chaco Canyon and Tsegi Canyon, seem to have immigrated here, although probably not staying for long. In the 1200s, the population of Canyon de Chelly was in decline, and by 1284, Mummy Cave, the last occupied village in the canyon, was vacant. Was drought the cause? Possibly, and yet the Canyon de Chelly people had successfully survived earlier dry periods; Antelope House was actually abandoned during a period of abundant rainfall. The subject of abandonment is complex and perhaps the proponents of cliff-dwellings-for-defense are right—an enemy appeared, causing warfare and flight.

There is some evidence that the Hopi Indians visited Canyon de Chelly after A.D. 1300 and perhaps even established summer or year-round residences. Hopi legends, as well as ceramic evidence, also support this theory. There is a logic to the Hopi connection, since the Hopi Mesas were one of the places to which refugees from the Four Corners region migrated in the late 1200s.

Navajos, a nomadic Apachean people, migrated into the Southwest from the Great Plains in the fifteenth and sixteenth centuries and began inhabiting Canyon de Chelly around 1700. As the Rio Grande Valley became colonized by Spaniards (1598–1821) and later fell under the rule of Mexico (1821–1846) and ultimately was occupied by the United States, Canyon de Chelly became a Navajo stronghold. From here, Navajo war parties staged devastating raids upon settlers who were moving westward from the Rio Grande Valley and encroaching on traditional Navajo territory. In 1805, a punitive expedition under Lt. Antonio Narbona entered Canyon de Chelly and fought an all-day battle with a band of Navajos trapped in Massacre Cave, a rock shelter. One hundred

White House ruins, Canyon de Chelly.

Navajo pictograph of Spanish horsemen, Canyon del Muerto.

fifteen Indians were killed. A dramatic Navajo pictograph above Standing Cow Ruins is believed to depict the Narbona expedition.

One of the last military conflicts between Navajos and Anglo-Americans occurred in 1864 when Col. Kit Carson led a detachment of cavalry into Canyon de Chelly, overwhelmed Navajo forces, and burned their homes and crops. With Indian resistance broken, the American army forcibly moved more than 8,000 Navajos to Fort Sumner in eastern New Mexico. Here they remained captive for several years before being marched back to their homeland. The experience, in which hundreds perished, is known as The Long Walk.

Approximately 300 Navajos now live in Canyon de Chelly and Canyon del Muerto from May to October, when they farm, tend their orchards, and keep flocks of sheep. Their hogans and corrals can be spotted from various points along the canyon rim. Visitors who enter the canyon should remember that the whole area, even though a national monument, is also private property.

A good way to see Canyon de Chelly is to follow the twenty-two-mile Rim Drive and stop at its scenic overlooks. You will see cliff dwellings and farms and will be moved by the beauty of the miniature landscape below. From White House Overlook, just over six miles from monument headquarters, a two-and-a-half mile round-trip hiking trail leads to White House ruins, the home of about a hundred Anasazi Indians from about A.D. 1060 to 1275. This hike, which involves climbing 500 feet in and out of the canyon and wading across the river, takes one and a half to two hours. It is the only excursion into the canyon that non-Navajo visitors may do on their own. The park service, however, offers other walking tours at scheduled times.

Visitors wishing to enter the canyons for a closer look at the cliff dwellings, rock art panels, and Navajo farms have two options. Many elect to take a commercial half- or full-day tour in an open bus offered by Thunderbird Lodge, located near the visitor center. Others use their own four-wheel-drive vehicles and engage the paid services of a Navajo guide through the park service. Horseback trips also can be arranged.

Facilities at the monument include a visitor center, picnic sites, north- and south-rim driving loops, and a campground. Overnight accommodations and a cafeteria are available at Thunderbird Lodge. Other travel services are found in the town of Chinle. Public visitation at Canyon de Chelly has greatly increased in recent years, so reservations often are needed well in advance.

From Canyon de Chelly, travelers can drive to a viewpoint overlooking Three Turkey Ruins outside the monument. To get there, continue to a pulloff beyond Spider Rock Overlook. Other interesting places to visit in the area are Hubbell Trading Post National Historic Site and the villages of the Hopi Indians.

> Suggested reading: *Canyon de Chelly: Its People and Rock Art*, by Campbell Grant, University of Arizona Press, Tucson, Arizona, 1978.

Grand Canyon National Park

Grand Canyon National Park is accessible from its south or north rims. The South Rim is located along Arizona 64, 57 miles north of Interstate 40 at Williams, Arizona. The North Rim headquarters are at the end of Arizona 67, 44 miles south of Jacob Lake. The North Rim is closed from about mid-October to about mid-May.

Grand Canyon is a picture window into time past. Its many layers of colorful rock, descending thousands of feet to the Colorado River, symbolize the hours of a regressive clock whose hands move slower than the human mind can comprehend. Within its long hour of geologic time, Grand Canyon's human story accounts for but seconds.

Archaeologists have discovered a rare type of artifact buried in cysts within the recesses of certain canyon caves. Known as "split-twig figurines," these rare objects are small effigies of mountain sheep, carefully crafted of split and twisted willow and cottonwood twigs, sometimes in combination with grass or bark. A few have been found pierced by miniature spears or with a dung pellet pushed into their cavities. The figurines probably were magic objects that played a part in the rituals of hunters who long ago roamed the canyons and mesas of Arizona. They are thought to be about 4,000 years old, thus predating Tutankhamen's rule of Egypt.

Small groups of Basketmaker people began using the Grand Canyon about A.D. 500, and by A.D. 700, a few Anasazi farming settlements had been established on the South Rim. Within two centuries, the North Rim was settled. This tentative population grew steadily over the next several centuries.

About A.D. 1050, large numbers of Anasazi began to establish communities on its rims and plateaus and near arable deltas in the inner canyon. Increased rainfall at this time enhanced farming in the hot arid environment along the Colorado River. Very likely, the new settlers alternated seasonally between living on the rims and within the canyons. With a 5,600-foot elevation differential from canyon bottom to rim, these areas would have lengthened their overall growing season and allowed them to produce enough food to survive.

While the Anasazi were living at Grand Canyon, another somewhat enigmatic group also was in the region—the Cohonina. Frankly, little can be said about these people, however, some archaeologists believe they lived in the region between about A.D. 700 and 1100 and possibly moved here from the south; indeed, the word Cohonina means "people who came from the south" in the Hopi language. Scholars still know little about their origins and culture and debate whether they more resembled the hunter-gatherers or the farmers.

Archaeologists have identified many sites in the Grand Canyon that were inhabited between A.D. 1050 and 1150. This period, at least until modern times, represents the climax of the canyon's human story. By A.D. 1200 or so, the Anasazi had departed from the Grand Canyon, never to return. They migrated eastward, probably to the area of the Hopi Mesas. Oraibi, a present-day Hopi village on Third Mesa, was founded about A.D. 1200, and until recent times, the Hopi Indians returned regularly to the Grand Canyon to collect salt and visit a shrine along the Little Colorado River. This shrine is a mineral spring that they believe to be the Sipapu or original place of emergence in the present era of human and animal life.

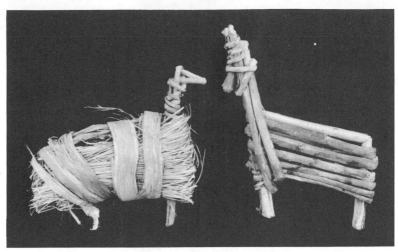

Split-willow twig figurines from a Grand Canyon cave.

Another group of Indians at Grand Canyon in prehistoric and historic times were the Kaibab Paiutes, who migrated into the region about A.D. 1400. Typically, an extended Paiute family or group of several families would roam around hunting and gathering what they needed to eat in environments ranging from hot dry deserts to high cool forests. They followed a seasonal cycle, exploiting a wide variety of plants as their fruits and seeds matured. The Paiutes made their shelters of upright poles and matted branches, sometimes making circular enclosures of pine boughs. In winter, they took shelter in caves. Early Paiute culture resembled that of the Archaic people who lived some thousands of years earlier. In the early nineteenth century, many Kaibab Paiutes were taken captive in a thriving southwestern slave trade. One eyewitness reported that they were "hunted in the spring of the year, when weak and helpless, by a certain class of men, and when taken, are fattened, carried to Santa Fe and sold as slaves during their minority" (Kelly and Fowler, 1986). Following the slaving era, traditional Paiute territory was encroached upon increasingly by European-American settlers, and the Indians were submitted to generations of mistreatment under a mismanaged reservation system.

Three archaeological sites in and around the canyon have been excavated and opened to visitors. Tusayan Ruin, located on the South Rim along the well-traveled road between Grand Canyon Village and Desert View, is a small, unimposing ruin consisting of a few room walls and the remains of a kiva. Tusayan was built in the last decade or two of the 1100s. This pueblo, which housed about thirty people, thrived after the main Anasazi occupation of Grand Canyon and only survived for about two generations. Perhaps its inhabitants were among the last stragglers to pick up their belongings and seek a better life elsewhere.

Tusayan originally consisted of a U-shaped room block with eight living units plus storage rooms and a kiva. When the latter was burned, another was built on the village trash mound a short distance from the plaza. This kiva can be viewed today along the interpretive ruins trail. The trash mound site apparently was chosen to give the kiva greater depth since bedrock lies only inches beneath the ground. The kiva, nevertheless, was poorly constructed out of slanting wall timbers with upright posts supporting a brushwork and dirt roof. Both kivas were excavated in the 1930s by the noted archaeologist Emil W. Haury.

Tusayan Ruin can be seen at any time of day, following a short self-guided trail. The site includes an interpretive trail and a small museum with a reconstruction of how the pueblo might have looked about A.D. 1185. The museum is open daily throughout the year and offers a schedule of talks on Grand Canyon prehistory.

The Walhalla Glades Ruin on the North Rim is located across the road from the Walhalla Glades Overlook, 24 miles from Grand Canyon Lodge and two miles from Cape Royal. It is an excavated, stabilized, and interpreted site consisting of a small house that probably sheltered a single family after A.D. 1050. Archaeological investigations were conducted here and at other nearby sites in 1969 and 1970 by the School of American Research.

Although some Basketmaker artifacts have been found on the Walhalla Plateau, the Anasazi probably did not live here in significant numbers until the 900s when settlers built scattered field houses to store grain and live in seasonally. By the mid-1000s, however, the population here greatly increased. The North Rim, at an elevation of over 8,000 feet, experienced severe winters with large snow accumulations that provided ground moisture for favorable late-spring plantings. Still, the growing seasons were short, and when cool weather arrived, the Anasazi returned to their inner canyon homes to plant fall crops and spend the winter.

The first written report on Grand Canyon archaeology was made by John Wesley Powell on his famous expedition down the Colorado in 1869. One of the sites he mentioned was Bright Angel Pueblo, located along the Kaibab Trail about a hundred yards from the north end of the Colorado River footbridge. This site is readily accessible to hikers. Its former occupants built a pithouse here about A.D. 1050 but were forced away by drought fifteen years later. About 1100, several families moved back to the site and built a small pueblo. They hunted and gathered, raised vegetables, and carried on the normal seasonal maintenance chores of inner-canyon living. They were able to sustain themselves in

Tusayan Ruin, Grand Canyon National Park.

this manner until about 1140, when they joined most other Grand Canyon Anasazi in a general exodus from the region. Trail distances to Bright Angel Pueblo by way of the Kaibab or Bright Angel trails are seven and nine miles, respectively; it is a fourteen-mile hike from the North Rim. Camping and overnight accommodations are available by reservation at nearby Phantom Ranch.

No commentary on Grand Canyon's human history should omit mention of the Havasupai Indians, who have lived in the western section of the canyon along Havasu Creek for untold generations. In prehistoric and early historic times, Havasupai life in the canyon and on the South Rim was not dissimilar to

View of Grand Canyon from South Rim.

that of the Anasazi centuries before. Today, they lead a quiet rural life in their isolated valley—the last community in North America to receive regular mail delivery by mule train. People interested in visiting the Havasupai Reservation and staying at the tribal lodge or campground should call (602) 448-2121 for further information.

The Grand Canyon of the Colorado is one of the world's great natural wonders, a geologic and scenic phenomenon of stunning magnitude. It is only in fairly recent times that the region's human past has been seriously studied. This research gap is due in part to the understandable fascination by scientists with the area's natural history. But in addition, this is no easy region in which to conduct archaeology. Environmental and topographical obstacles are formidable enough to give even the most ardent and well-equipped archaeologists second thoughts. Excavation crews at Unkar Delta in the late 1960s, for example, depended on helicopters for food and supplies, which added immensely to the project's cost. These stalwart diggers worked for months in virtual isolation in an area that afforded no natural shelter from high winds and where daytime temperatures sometimes soared to 120 degrees. It is no wonder that archaeology in the Grand Canyon lagged somewhat behind that in other more welcoming areas. For that matter, anyone who has hiked through the canyon can appreciate the fact that this was an Anasazi frontier, where life was tenuous and thriving villages of one decade might lie as silent ghost towns the next.

> Suggested reading: *On the Edge of Splendor: Exploring Grand Canyon's Human Past,* by Douglas W. Schwartz, School of American Research, Santa Fe, New Mexico, 1989; "Southern Paiute," by Isabel T. Kelly and Catherine S. Fowler, in *Handbook of North American Indians,* vol. 11, edited by Warren L. D'Azevedo, Smithsonian Institution, Washington, D.C., 1986.

Homol'ovi Ruins State Park

Homol'ovi Ruins State Park is located just north of Winslow, Arizona. To reach the park, take the exit at Winslow from Interstate 40 onto Arizona 87 and continue 1 mile to the park entrance on the left.

People visiting many ruins in the northern part of the Southwest learn that in the late 1200s the Anasazi abandoned the Four Corners region and migrated east to the Rio Grande and south to the Hopi Mesas and Little Colorado River. Archaeologists believe Homol'ovi, situated along the Little Colorado River, is one of the sites inhabited by these immigrants.

The five pueblo ruins at Homol'ovi Ruins State Park are located in open country and consist of mounds, some of which have been extensively pothunted. A new visitor center and museum is located at the Homol'ovi II ruins, which are just off Interstate 40 in Winslow. This site is the principal attraction in the park, but visitors may also go to the other Homol'ovi ruins and follow a trail down the mesa to see a series of petroglyphs. From the ruins, you can look down over the Little Colorado River and enjoy a view that stretches to the Hopi Buttes and San Francisco Peaks. Your first view of the ruins may bring to mind a cratered battlefield. The craters are holes dug by pothunters; a treasure trove of material was evidently stolen from this site over the years. The holes, however, only penetrate the upper story of the pueblo, and archaeologists plan to excavate portions of the lower story in hopes of salvaging information about the Anasazi people who occupied the pueblo.

The first excavations at Homol'ovi were by Jesse Walter Fewkes in 1896. Fewkes was particularly interested in the site's connection with the nearby Hopi Indians. He learned from the Hopis that Homol'ovi was one of their ancestral sites. The Hopis knew which clans had occupied it and had oral traditions relating to

Petroglyph at Homol'ovi State Park.

its founding and eventual abandonment. Archaeological material at the ruins reinforced the oral history.

Since 1984, archaeologists from the Arizona State Museum have been excavating the Homol'ovi ruins. According to E. Charles Adams, director of the research project, and his colleagues, Anasazi Indians lived in a number of small pithouse hamlets around Homol'ovi between A.D. 750 and 850, a relatively wet period. The people apparently were carrying out some farming in the sand dunes without irrigation. Since this is a relatively unproductive method of agriculture, researchers speculate Homol'ovi's first occupants may only have been living here on a seasonal basis.

When the weather turned drier about A.D. 850, the Homol'ovi people moved elsewhere, possibly north to the Hopi Buttes area, but they returned 200 years later to reestablish pithouse hamlets and continue dry farming. Still, their numbers were small. After A.D. 1250, however, the population at Homol'ovi began to swell. At least seven small hamlets were established on the east side of the river, and soon after 1275, two pueblos, Homol'ovi III and IV, were founded on the west side. The immigrants, who came from the Hopi Buttes area to the north and the Mogollon Rim to the south, were drawn to Homol'ovi by the availability of water and farmlands.

Soon after A.D. 1300, the west bank sites were abandoned, their residents moving across the river. This move apparently motivated the east bank inhabitants to consolidate, perhaps with the newcomers, into larger pueblos including Homol'ovi I, with 250 rooms, and Homol'ovi II, with over 700 rooms. Some still returned to Homol'ovi III seasonally to farm. Cotton seems to have been cultivated extensively along the Little Colorado and was traded with distant pueblos for pottery, especially yellow ware from the Hopi. The Homol'ovi people farmed intensively in the floodplain of the river, in the dunes, in the valleys, and in more upland areas where they diverted runoff water to their crops. As population grew, the society became more organized, especially in the way it controlled land use. Inhabitants planned their villages around a central plaza, which was probably used for religious ceremonies. After A.D. 1325, the iconography of pottery decorations and rock art reflects the appearance of the kachina cult, a complex of religious practices that is still active among the Hopis and other Pueblo Indians. Sometime in the early 1400s, after more than a hundred years of intensive occupation, Homol'ovi was abandoned for good.

In 1991, Homol'ovi was officially opened as a state park, with an interpretive program based on the recent years of archaeological research. As long as these excavations continue in the summers, visitors will be able to watch archaeologists at work on the site. No ruins in the Southwest more poignantly demonstrates the havoc that pothunting can wreak upon an archaeological site. When this happens, a portion of our American history and heritage is lost, and a sense of injury is felt by the Native American descendants of the people whose graves have been disturbed.

Homol'ovi Ruins State Park has a campground, and a variety of travel services are available in the town of Winslow. Visitors heading west on Interstate 40 may enjoy stopping at Walnut Canyon National Monument (see p. 153) and Elden Pueblo (see p. 146) in Flagstaff.

Suggested reading: *Kiva*, Vol. 54, No. 3, Arizona Archaeological and Historical Society, Tucson, Arizona, 1989.

Petrified Forest National Park

Petrified Forest National Park is located along Interstate 40, 25 miles east of Holbrook, Arizona, and also along U.S. 180, 19 miles east of Holbrook.

Petrified Forest, in east-central Arizona, has the largest and most colorful collection of fossilized trees in the world. In this unique desert park, you can walk through a series of "forests" where giant agate logs litter the surface of the ground, relics of an age that antedates by millions of years the presence of human beings in the Southwest. This desolate region, the beauty of which lies in the rich colorations of its arid sands and clays, does not seem to hold much potential for sustaining life. But on its mesas and around ancient springs and seeps, many small Basketmaker and Pueblo villages, as well as abundant collec-tions of prehistoric petroglyphs, testify to a long human history in the region. Indeed, even the petrified wood, which we regard as an antediluvian curiosity, served a practical purpose to the Anasazi who lived here.

There is some evidence that Archaic hunter-gatherers had ephemeral camps in the Petrified Forest area as long ago as 1000 B.C. or earlier. By A.D. 300 to 500, a few early Basketmaker people were living in the region, probably on a seasonal basis. They lived in shallow, slab-lined pithouses with dome-like roofs of sticks, brush, and mud supported by poles. There is evidence that these early settlers may have migrated here from the Mogollon area to the south, as well as from the north. By A.D. 700, small villages probably were being used year-round as their residents developed more efficient and productive methods of farming. However, it was not for another 200 or 300 years that the population of the region became significant, as evidenced by a proliferation of small pueblos.

The Puerco Ruin, founded about A.D. 1250, is the largest site in the park and, conveniently, is situated along the Mainline Road. Its initial occupants may have migrated here from drought-stricken areas during the latter part of the thirteenth century. Twenty-five of the site's 125 rooms have been excavated and stabilized over the years and are easily accessible to visitors. This one-story pueblo, which overlooks the Puerco River, was designed in a rectangular form, 230 by 180 feet in dimensions, surrounding an interior plaza with three kivas. Its maximum population probably reached about 200 people, who sustained themselves by farming the floodplains along the river, as well as hunting rabbits, prairie dogs, and other game and gathering wild plants. The abundance of chipped stone artifacts, mostly

Petroglyphs at Petrified Forest National Park.

petrified wood, in and around the site has caused archaeologists to speculate that tool manufacture was a central activity here. Imported pottery found here and at other Petrified Forest sites shows that these Anasazi traded with the ancestors of the Hopis and Zunis, as well as with the inhabitants of towns such as Kinishba (see p. 106) in the White Mountains to the south. Homol'ovi Pueblo (see p. 101) also was active at the same time.

Parts of Puerco Pueblo were abandoned and filled with trash prior to a final hurried departure from the village, at which time its occupants set fire to their living and store rooms. Archaeological remains, however, do not shed further light on the circumstances surrounding the abandonment of this site.

A special attraction of the Puerco Ruin is the large collection of petroglyphs scattered on rocks and boulders around the south and east sides of the mesa. Numbering more than 800, they include representations of human figures, animals, birds, kachina masks, and geometric designs. In addition, two smaller clusters of glyphs can be found across Mainline Road on the opposite side of the mesa, and farther down the road at Newspaper Rock, a large panel can be viewed. Other rock art sites in the park may be visited with special permission from the park service.

Another easily accessible pueblo site, in the southern end of the park, is Agate House. Reconstructed in 1934, this small pueblo was built of chunks of petrified wood.

Petrified Forest was first reported in 1851 by Lt. Lorenzo Sitgreaves while on a U.S. Army exploratory expedition in northern Arizona. Six years later, the region was traversed by Lt. Beale's legendary camel caravan en route to California. After the building of the railroad in the 1880s, this bleak country saw an influx of tourists, souvenir hunters, and gem collectors. The conservationist John Muir excavated at the Puerco Ruin in 1905–1906. Muir was concerned by the environmental impact of a nearby stamp mill, which was crushing petrified logs into abrasives, and helped convince President Theodore Roosevelt to declare Petrified Forest a national monument in 1906. It was the country's second national monument.

To obtain more detailed information on Petrified Forest, its geology, and cultural history, visitors should stop at the visitor center and museum. The main road through the park passes near most of the more interesting fossil wood and archaeological sites. The nearest travel services are in Holbrook.

Suggested reading: *Archaeological Investigations at Puerco Ruins, Petrified Forest National Park, Arizona,* by Jeffery F. Burton, U.S. Department of the Interior, Publications in Anthropology 54, Washington, D.C., 1990.

Kinishba Ruins

To find Kinishba Ruins, drive 15 miles west of Whiteriver, Arizona, on Arizona 73 to the Kinishba Ruins sign on the highway. Turn right and continue about 4 miles to the ruins, which are signed.

Like so many important archaeological sites in the Southwest, Kinishba was first reported in the early 1880s by the anthropologist and historian Adolph F. Bandelier. Half a century later, after much pothunting at the site by soldiers stationed at nearby Fort Apache, a large portion of Kinishba was excavated and restored by a crew of University of Arizona students and Apache Indians under the supervision of Byron Cummings. Much of the original pueblo, however, has never fallen prey to the archaeologist's shovel or trowel and remains as overgrown mounds.

The Kinishba villagers were farmers who cultivated corn, beans, and squash on arable lands sloping southeast to the White River. They lived here between about A.D. 1050 and 1350, a period when Anasazi culture was vigorous and expansive.

Cummings selected Kinishba for excavation because it represented, in his own words, "the highest development of the Pueblo culture." The wealth of artifacts that he collected here during

Kinishba.

nine summers of field work testify to the highly developed craft skills of the Anasazi. The collection also demonstrates the heterogeneous character of Kinishba's culture; its inhabitants exchanged ideas and trade goods with Kayenta Anasazi people to the north, Tularosa people to the east, the Hopi villages of Sikyatki and Awatavi, and Salado and Hohokam communities of the lower Salt and Gila drainages to the south.

Kinishba was a large masonry pueblo consisting of several substantial community houses; one of these was the focus of the 1930s project. The pueblo was constructed on top of an older collapsed village, and numerous pithouses in the area give a clue to an even older local Basketmaker occupation. Prehistoric southwestern peoples had a propensity for reoccupying previously inhabited sites, often building new homes on top of the ruins of older structures. Kinishba's room blocks were well built and compact. The excavated wing had over 200 rooms, and the entire pueblo may have had a population of 1,500 to 2,000 people. Cummings was of the opinion that this large, productive, long-lived village must have had strong social organization and effective leadership.

At the end of Cummings's scientific investigations of Kinishba, he built a research and exhibition complex that he envisioned as the core of a model educational park. He hoped that, in time, professional and lay people would come here to tour the ruins, relax under shade trees in a park, view Kinishba art and artifacts in a modern museum, and enjoy a contemporary Native American craft center.

Regrettably, World War II shifted funding away from projects like this and public interest drifted away from Cummings's plan. Today, Kinishba is fenced off, deteriorating, barely known to the public, and visited by few. To the serious archaeology student, however, it represents an important example of Western Pueblo culture and is far from forgotten.

Kinishba Ruins are administered by the Fort Apache Tribe, which does not require permission to visit the site. When you go there, you are pretty much on your own and will find no interpretation or facilities.

Suggested reading: *Kinishba: A Prehistoric Pueblo of the Great Pueblo Period*, by Byron Cummings, The University of Arizona, Tucson, Arizona, 1940.

Casamero Ruins

To reach Casamero Ruins, take Exit 63 off Interstate 40 at Prewitt, New Mexico. A short distance east of the exit junction with U.S. 66, McKinley County Road 19 leads north to the Plains Escalante Generating Station. Follow this road 4 miles to a small parking area on the left, which is next to the ruins.

Casamero is one of Chaco Canyon's (see p. 119) many *outliers*, a term referring to ruins with characteristic Chacoan features and that thrived when Chaco's influence was at its peak in the eleventh and twelfth centuries. Other examples of Chacoan outliers in this guidebook are Salmon (see p. 131), Aztec (see p. 127), Escalante (see p. 46), and Chimney Rock (see p. 134) ruins. Chaco Canyon is fifty miles north of Casamero but some other outliers have been found even farther from the center. Frequently, "roads" lead to them from Chaco Canyon or from other outliers. Two of these roads are present at Casamero, one leading to a site east across Casamero Draw and the other heading west from a point south of the great kiva. The purpose of these roads has long been debated, and although theories abound, archaeologists have yet to reach a consensus on how and why they were used. Most researchers, however, lean toward a religious or ceremonial interpretation.

Whether the influence of the culture centered at Chaco Canyon outliers such as Casamero was political, economic, religious, or all of the above, it is often speculated (reasonably but without

Kiva entrance at Casamero ruins.

proof) that the sites' great houses, with their Chacoan design and masonry, were the residences of important individuals or families from Chaco Canyon. At Casamero you can see the typical Chacoan "banded masonry" construction, which is identifiable by its large horizonally laid blocks of sandstone and limestone alternating with thin bands of chinking. Other Chacoan clues are enclosed kivas and separate great kivas, both of which are present at Casamero.

Chacoan outliers typically are surrounded by many small pueblos and farmsteads. If an overlord resided in the great house, he probably exerted some power over the Anasazi peasants living nearby. Casamero is situated on a grassy slope in the shadow of massive red sandstone cliffs overlooking a broad valley. The Anasazi tilled their fields in the valley and, when they departed, left many small pueblos and farmsteads behind them. Subsequently, Navajos farmed and herded sheep in the valley, and their sites, too, are part of the archaeological picture. Some Navajos apparently left the area only a few generations ago under pressure from Anglo-American ranchers.

The Casamero great house, which was occupied between A.D. 1000 and 1125, contains twenty-two ground-floor rooms and probably had some second-story rooms on its west side. The stabilized walls of the pueblo stand about waist high, and you can walk freely about the site. Two hundred feet southeast of the pueblo is the unexcavated great kiva, which appears as a large shallow depression. Its diameter is conservatively estimated at seventy feet, making it almost twice the size of the great kiva at Aztec Ruins and even larger than the one at Casa Rinconada in Chaco Canyon. While Casamero is a smallish pueblo, the size of the great kiva hints at the large prehistoric population of the valley.

Casamero was excavated between 1966 and 1975 and subsequently stabilized by the Bureau of Land Management to protect its walls and better prepare the site for visitors. Extensive archaeological investigations were carried out in the vicinity in the late 1970s by the School of American Research to obtain clearance for construction of a nearby coal-fired electrical generating plant. This plant and its smoke plume are clearly visible from the ruins, creating a poignant contrast between ancient and modern worlds. The investigations revealed more than 140 archaeological sites in the vicinity, ranging from Basketmaker pithouses and Pueblo structures from the eleventh century and earlier to twentieth-century Navajo hogans, ramadas, sheep pens, and sweat lodges.

The Bureau of Land Management administers Casamero as a Chaco Culture Archaeological Protection Site and has installed several helpful interpretive signs among the ruins. The bureau requests the public's assistance in reporting any stealing or vandalism that visitors may witness at the site to its Farmington office (505) 327-5344. The nearest travel services are in Grants and Milan, twenty miles east on Interstate 40, and in Gallup, forty miles to the west. Other nearby ruins are the Dittert Site (opposite) and Chaco Canyon (see p. 119).

Suggested reading: *Anasazi Communities of the San Juan Basin,* by Michael P. Marshall, et al., Albuquerque Photo Lab, Albuquerque, New Mexico, 1979.

The Dittert Site

The Dittert Site is located several miles east of New Mexico 117, 42 miles south of Grants, New Mexico. To reach the ruin, drive 5 miles east of Grants on Interstate 40, then continue 9 miles south on New Mexico 117 to the Bureau of Land Management ranger station, where further directions to the site may be obtained.

When tourists and travelers think of Indian ruins, usually what first comes to mind are dramatic celebrity sites such as Cliff Palace at Mesa Verde, Pueblo Bonito at Chaco Canyon, and Montezuma Castle in the Verde Valley. These ruins are, indeed, the stars of southwestern prehistory, and visits to them are usually shared with dozens or scores of others under the watchful eye of a park ranger.

The Dittert Site, by contrast, which has only recently been opened up to the public by the Bureau of Land Management, is an example of one of the more numerous and architecturally humble ruins that dot the southwestern landscape. Sites like this are well known to archaeologists and familiar to hikers who tramp through the region's remote canyons and across its solitary mesas. Alas, they are also known to the selfish few bent on stealing cultural antiquities. But to people on a tight sightseeing itinerary, ruins like the Dittert Site hold small attraction.

Unlike Cliff Palace and Montezuma Castle, the Dittert Site was named for the archaeologist who excavated it in the late 1940s, Alfred E. Dittert. Tree-ring samples that he collected at the site span the time period between A.D. 1226 and 1267. Since dendrochronology represents the most accurate archaeological dating method, we can safely assume that the Anasazi lived here in those years. But this thirteenth-century pueblo was built on an earlier mound, and future archaeological testing may show that its history goes back still another couple of centuries. Why its inhabitants left is not known. Perhaps they overexploited the natural resources in the vicinity, making it necessary to move on. They may have used up all the nearby wood for fuel and building, for example, or hunted out most of the deer and other game. Alternately, intensive agriculture over the seasons may eventually have depleted their garden plots.

Archaeologists have discussed whether or not the Dittert Site was an outlier of Chaco Canyon (see p. 119), since it has several Chacoan characteristics, including masonry style, kiva features, and even segments of a prehistoric road. Despite this evidence, however, the tree-ring dates, which fall substantially after the collapse of the Chacoan system (A.D. 1130–1175), suggest a post-Chacoan occupation.

The Dittert Site has over thirty rooms and one kiva. Alfred Dittert excavated and backfilled only eight rooms and the kiva, and today, the site appears as a substantial mound with several low-standing room walls made of sandstone blocks. The plaza was located in front of the kiva, outside the L-shaped room block. Archaeologists have found the ruins of numerous other smaller pueblos and farmsteads and a great kiva in the immediate vicinity, suggesting that the village was the focus of a substantial prehistoric community.

How did these Native Americans subsist? Their homes were situated at the foot of a slope leading up Cebolleta Mesa and look out over vast expanses of prairie to the south. Thus, its inhabitants would have been able to hunt and gather plants in both the nearby grasslands and scrub woodlands. Of even more importance, Armijo Canyon and other drainages spilled out their waters from the uplands behind the pueblo to create favorable agricultural areas and provide relatively stable water sources. Two miles up the canyon is a spring that probably could have been counted on for water during dry spells. More resources would have been available at a somewhat greater walking distance on the Malpais (badlands) to the west. Also to the west, a corridor between the Malpais and Cebolleta Mesa would have served as a natural travel and trade corridor of economic and social advantage to the Dittert residents.

The protection and public interpretation of ancient ruins has long been the province of the National Park Service. In recent years, however, both the U.S. Forest Service and the Bureau of Land Management have joined in this effort, a move reflecting their new-found interest in "recreational" programs (cultural resources fall under the recreational heading) to complement their traditional role of leasing natural resources to private mining, oil drilling, and logging companies. The Dittert Site is one example of archaeological ruins that the Bureau of Land Management has recently made available to the public.

Another "new" ruin that may interest readers traveling from the southwest is Casa Malpais in Springerville, Arizona (see p. 12). The new Malpais National Monument south of Grants is also of interest, especially since it includes the historic Zuni-Acoma trail, an ancient Indian trail across the badlands. The nearest travel services are in Grants and Quemado.

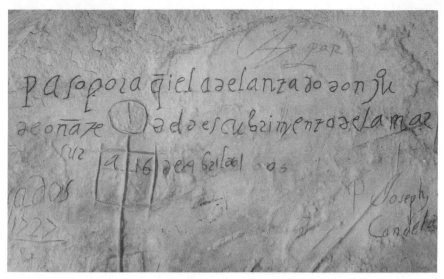

A famous message left at Inscription Rock: "Passed by here the Adelantado Don Juan de Oñate, from the discovery of the Sea of the South, the 16th of April of 1605."

El Morro National Monument

El Morro National Monument is located on New Mexico 53, 40 miles west of Grants and 30 miles east of Zuni, New Mexico.

The Atsinna ruin, an ancestral Zuni fortified pueblo perched on top of El Morro Mesa, has a bird's-eye view over the upper valley of the Zuni River. Below the site is Inscription Rock, resembling the prow of a great stone ship, which bears the carved names of conquistadores, explorers, and settlers, some famous, others known only by their signatures. At the base of the *morro*, which means "bluff" or "headland" in Spanish, a large pool collects runoff from the mesa. It was a useful camping spot for Indians and Spaniards traveling from the Zuni pueblos to the Rio Grande Valley. While they rested, they would inscribe their names, often with the date and a comment, on the base of the rock. Thus, over hundreds of years, an intriguing folk-historic register was created.

Paleo and Archaic hunter-gatherers knew this region many thousands of years ago, but real settlement did not begin until after A.D. 400, as evidenced by pithouse villages downriver from El Morro, near Zuni. In the mid-1200s, Pueblo Indians in the Zuni area apparently were coping with drought conditions and decided that it would be to their benefit to move to the higher elevations of El Morro, which had greater rainfall.

The settlers established seven communities, each consisting of up to thirty separate small house groups spaced close to each other. Each of these clusters had at least one site situated on a high point with a view over the valley, the total population of which reached an estimated 3,000 to 4,000 people. However, these communities were short-lived, for sometime about A.D. 1275 to 1300, the Indians abandoned them to build larger, consolidated sites like Atsinna on top of the mesas.

Atsinna has more than 500 rooms. Its exterior walls have no entrances, and from their ramparts, sentries could have surveyed the entire valley, keeping watch on nearby pueblos. Atsinna's plan around a central courtyard meant that access could only be gained by ladders scaling the outermost walls. A defensive posture such as Atsinna's suggests that hostile conditions prevailed. Why? Here, the science of archaeology becomes even more speculative: Perhaps food was in short supply, and villages were trying to raid each other's stores.

An interesting sidelight to Atsinna was discovered by Steven LeBlanc, who did archaeological research in this area. LeBlanc discovered that a pueblo site across the valley was an almost exact architectural duplicate of Atsinna. Each pueblo was apparently planned as a complete unit, constructed in a single building period, then occupied by its residents, like an apartment complex today.

In the early 1300s, the residents of Atsinna and five other similar communities moved back downriver to their original territory near Zuni. The regional population, however, had experienced a decline over the past several generations. When the people returned to Zuni, they founded or resettled the six pueblos that Coronado encountered 250 years later. One of these was Hawikuh (see p. 116), which the Spaniards stormed in 1639; another was Halona, whose remains still underlie the old part of Zuni Pueblo.

A wing of Atsinna was excavated in the 1950s by the noted archaeologist Richard B. Woodbury and was later stabilized by the National Park Service. Woodbury reported that the inhabitants of the pueblo collected rainwater from natural rock basins and several reservoirs on the mesa. Also, the pool below would have been a good source of water, though it would have been tiresome to carry pots of water up the mesa.

To reach Atsinna, you need to climb up a steep footpath from the visitor center, but once at the top, the view itself is worth the effort. The trail takes you to a dozen or more excavated masonry

Atsinna Pueblo, El Morro National Monument.

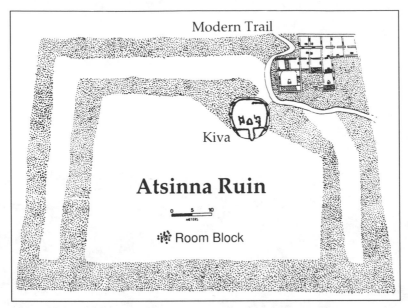

Plan of Atsinna.

rooms and two kivas. A site plan displays the pueblo's layout. From Atsinna, the trail continues across the mesa to a second undisturbed ruin, then descends the back side of the cliff and loops around to Inscription Rock. You should allow about an hour and a half for the complete hike.

El Morro is a particularly rewarding place to visit because it combines beautiful natural scenery with historical and prehistorical dimensions. The monument maintains an attractive picnic area and campground as well as a standard National Park Service visitor center. The nearest gas station is in Ramah, fifteen miles distant, and motels can be found in Grants or Gallup along Interstate 40. The National Forest Service also maintains campgrounds nearby. As an adjunct to El Morro, you may wish to visit Zuni Pueblo and arrange for a guided tour of Hawikuh and/or Village of the Great Kivas (see p. 125).

Suggested reading: *Zuni & El Morro: Past and Present*, edited by David Grant Noble, Ancient City Press, Santa Fe, New Mexico, 1993.

Hawikuh

The ruins of Hawikuh lie about 12 miles south of Zuni Pueblo in west-central New Mexico. Zuni is located on New Mexico 53, 35 miles south of Gallup and 71 miles west of Grants. To obtain permission to visit Hawikuh, call the Zuni Tribal Office at (505) 782-4481; for directions to the site, call the tribal archaeology department at 782-4814.

In 1539, a Spanish Moor named Estebanico, a scout for Fray Marcos de Niza, arrived at the Zuni pueblo of Hawikuh with a small group of Mexican Indians. It was the first encounter between any person from Europe and North Americans. Hawikuh was an impressive hilltop village, described by observers of the day as equal in size to Mexico City of that time. Hawikuh (also spelled Hawikku) is thought to have been founded about A.D. 1300 and was the Zuni's principal town until 1680, when it was aban-doned in the turmoil of the Great Pueblo Revolt. Zuni Indians, or *Ashiwi*, as they call themselves, still live in the vicinity of this historic site, which is on their reservation.

Archaeology shows that the Zunis of seven centuries ago were a people with complex social and political traditions who, in the words of one scholar, "compartmentalized an encyclopedic knowledge about the environment within the clans, kiva groups, curing societies, and priesthoods." In the late 1200s and early 1300s, the Zunis consolidated into large well-organized villages (see El Morro, p. 113), such as Hawikuh. Their territory, used for living, farming, hunting, gathering, and religious activity was much more extensive than today's reservation.

Such tribal strength was not anticipated by Estebanico when he approached Hawikuh. Fame and fortune at "discovering" what he presumed to be one of the Seven Golden Cities of Cibola may have dominated his thoughts. According to legend, Estebanico was a confident man with varied talents, a touch of flamboyance, a gift for languages, and a taste for women. Fame and fortune, however, were not to be his, since he was soon executed by the Zunis. Fray Marcos's party soon advanced to within sight of the pueblo, but having learned of Estebanico's misfortune, approached no closer. Perhaps the golden rays of the afternoon sun reflected off Hawikuh's high earthen walls and overly impressed the friar, for the report he submitted upon his return to Mexico City inspired another adventurer, Francisco Vasquez de Coronado, to organize a follow-up expedition.

Coronado and his army advanced up the west coast of Mexico in 1540, then turned east toward Zuni country. When they arrived at Hawikuh, they successfully stormed the pueblo, their superior force of arms providing a decisive advantage. Coronado himself was wounded in the battle. The expedition's chronicler later wrote, "We found what we needed more than gold and silver, and that was much corn, and beans and turkeys. . . ." After their arduous journey, the conquistadores ate well and rested as they occupied

Hawikuh. But, bitterly disappointed by the absence of precious metals in the pueblo, they soon pressed on eastward to the Rio Grande pueblos.

For forty years, the Zunis saw no more Spaniards, until 1581, when the Rodriguez-Chamiscado expedition reached their lands. These explorers received a warmer reception and even met three Mexican Indians whom Coronado had left behind. Zuni foreign policy had changed; now they emphasized hospitality over war, while urging the Europeans to travel farther on in their quests.

In 1629, Franciscan priests did establish a presence at Hawikuh and built a church here as well as one at Halona, a town twelve miles to the north at the site of the old section of present-day Zuni Pueblo. The Spaniards also instituted an Indian civil government based on the Spanish model. This imposed structure, however, was but a thin organizational veneer—the new Zuni "officials" still answered to their traditional council of priests.

The mission at Hawikuh was burned in 1632, rebuilt, burned and built again, and destroyed for the final time in the Pueblo Revolt of 1680. At this time, the Zunis abandoned Hawikuh altogether.

Archaeological excavations were carried out at Hawikuh by Frederick Webb Hodge in 1922–1923. Although Hodge confirmed that the site was inhabited as early as 1300, he was primarily interested in the period of Spanish-Indian contact, and he left earlier (deeper) levels of the site for later researchers to probe. Hodge neither backfilled nor stabilized his excavations, which resulted in the destruction of the exposed pueblo walls from weather. Here and there, portions of stone walls still stand, and the ill-fated church site is recognizable. But although these ruins are architecturally unimpressive today, the village is still striking by virtue of its size and commanding position. In addition, to stand upon the very spot where, 450 years ago, the Spanish empire first confronted North Americans is an experience to stir the imagination.

Hawikuh is administered by the Zuni Indians, who are interested in their history and support an active archaeology program on tribal lands. Someday, Hawikuh may be developed into a national monument, but this project is presently still under discussion. When you visit the site today, plan at least an hour and a half excursion from Zuni Pueblo. You may also arrange for your Zuni guide to take you to Village of the Great Kivas (see p. 125), a Chacoan ruin on another part of the reservation.

Zuni Pueblo has eating places, gas stations, grocery stores, and a campground. The nearest motels are in Gallup, along Interstate 40.

The mounds of Hawikuh.

Suggested reading: "Zuni Prehistory and History to 1850," by Richard B. Woodbury, in *Handbook of North American Indians*, vol. 9, edited by Alfonso Ortiz, Smithsonian Institution, Washington, D.C., 1979.

Chaco Culture National Historical Park

Chaco Culture National Historical Park is located along New Mexico 57 between Farmington and Grants. To reach the park from the north, turn off New Mexico 44 at Blanco Trading Post and follow New Mexico 57 for 23 miles. From the south, turn on New Mexico 57 from U.S. 66 (Interstate 40) at Thoreau and proceed 64 miles to the entrance.

Driving along the road from Blanco Trading Post or Crownpoint to Chaco Canyon, you may well wonder how any community of human beings could have survived here in times past. The broad, rough, arid landscape, broken only by occasional dry washes, rock outcroppings, and distant mesas seems to contradict the possibility of a major culture once thriving here. And yet, while driving, you pass tire tracks branching off the road to Navajo homes. Wisps of cedar smoke curling into the air are proof that this seeming desert still nurtures people.

Finally, you enter Chaco Canyon, a shallow rift fifteen miles long and up to a mile wide, bordered on the north and south by long mesa cliffs. The valley is now deeply cut by the Chaco Wash, on either side of which lie the ruins of large multistoried masonry pueblos, some excavated and restored, others still mounds. In their ruined state, they seem to fulfill the inhospitable message of the surrounding environment, but as ruins, they also are evidence of a once-teeming life in the canyon. Here was an Anasazi cultural center with a population in the thousands and a sphere of influence extending up to a hundred miles in all directions. It is not surprising that what happened along the Chaco Wash 900 years ago is sometimes called "the Chaco phenomenon." And yet, after generations of archaeological investigations, the nature of that phenomenon still remains an enigma.

One of the early excavation projects was carried out between 1896 and 1899 by the Hyde Exploring Expedition at Pueblo Bonito. Since then, many institutions have sponsored research in the canyon, including the School of American Research, the University of New Mexico, the National Geographic Society, the Smithsonian Institution, and the National Park Service, which completed extensive investigations at Pueblo Alto as recently as 1980. While scientific data accumulates, many central questions remain. How was such a seemingly large community in the canyon sustained, given the meager local agricultural potential? Why have archaeologists found so few burials? How were the "roads" used that radiate in straight lines from the canyon to outlying communities? What role did the great pueblos of the canyon play in the network of Chacoan sites that extends thoughout the San Juan Basin? In short, why was Chaco Canyon what it was, and what was it?

Although nomadic native hunters and gatherers certainly knew Chaco Canyon as long as 10,000 years ago, the area's first real residents were Basketmakers, who lived at such sites as Atlatl Cave and Shabik'eshchee Village beginning about 900 B.C. The Basketmakers lived in the canyon many centuries before the appearance of early Pueblo people, with their characteristic small, one-storied, masonry pueblos, about A.D. 700.

About A.D. 900, population in the canyon was on the increase, and the Anasazi were beginning to build larger, more compact pueblos. One group of settlers was living in a curved row of rooms near the north wall of the canyon, the first section of what would grow to be the spectacular Pueblo Bonito. But the main building boom did not get under way until about 1030 when work appears to have accelerated at a frenzied pace.

Within a couple of generations, Chaco Canyon had become a power center in the Anasazi world. By A.D. 1115, some seventy

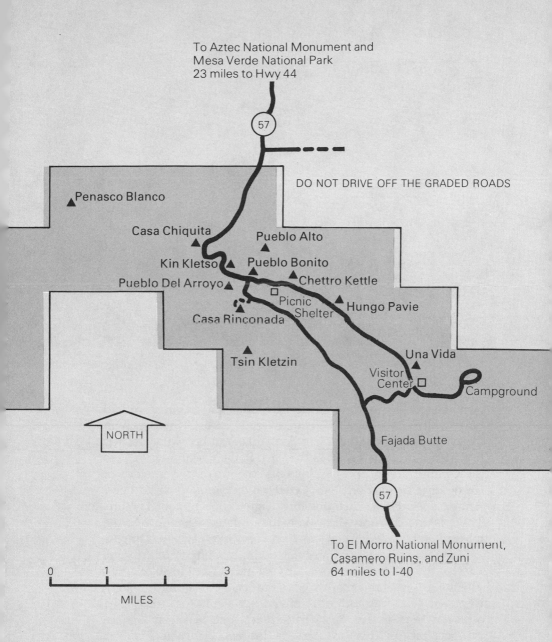

To Aztec National Monument and
Mesa Verde National Park
23 miles to Hwy 44

57

DO NOT DRIVE OFF THE GRADED ROADS

▲ Penasco Blanco

Casa Chiquita ▲

Kin Kletso ▲

Pueblo Alto ▲

Pueblo Bonito ▲

Pueblo Del Arroyo ▲

Chettro Kettle ▲

Picnic Shelter

Hungo Pavie ▲

Casa Rinconada ▲

Tsin Kletzin ▲

Una Vida ▲

Visitor Center

Campground

NORTH

Fajada Butte

57

To El Morro National Monument,
Casamero Ruins, and Zuni
64 miles to I-40

0   1   3

MILES

Chaco Canyon

Pueblo Bonito from above.

outlying pueblos with characteristic Chacoan architecture had
been built within the 25,000 square-mile area of the San Juan
Basin. The purpose of these so-called outliers and how they related
to Chaco Canyon is veiled in the past. Some researchers believe
they were trading posts. Others see them as the domiciles of
strong Chacoan overlords who taxed the surrounding populations.
And no one excludes their possible religious or ceremonial nature.
There is one certainty, however; they related somehow to the
magnificently designed and constructed pueblos of Chaco Canyon.

Many outliers were connected to Chaco Canyon and to one
another by "roads," some of which extended forty to sixty miles.
The full extent of this roadway system has been brought to light
in recent years through specialized aerial photography. One
aspect of the roads that most perplexes researchers is their configu-
ration; typically, they are shallow depressions, twenty-five to
forty feet wide, sometimes demarcated by rock edging or curbing.
Robert Powers, a leading Chacoan road expert, has written, "the
generally straight, undeviating bearings of the roads suggest that
they were laid out or 'engineered' prior to their actual construction." Some roads traverse steep cliffs by the use of handcut stairways; others reached mesa tops by climbing up massive handbuilt
earth and rock ramps. Powers speculates that the roads may have
accommodated certain types of foot processions or allowed trans-

Back wall of Chetro Ketl, Chaco Canyon.

portation of building materials but admits that archaeologists have not yet found any satisfying reason for the existence of the roads.

About A.D. 1140 the system began to fall apart. First the outliers were abandoned, and by the end of the century, the towns in Chaco Canyon were vacant as well. The collapse of the Chacoan system coincides with a period of drought; however, in all probability, other factors, which are not yet understood, also played a part in its demise.

More has been written about the Chacoans than could ever be summarized here. Studies have been published on their architecture, social organization, trade networks, roads, water control systems, religion, archaeoastronomy, and outlying communities. But at Chaco Canyon, it is the architecture that will be most immediately impressive. The name Pueblo Bonito is almost synonymous with Chaco Canyon, and visitors should give a priority to seeing this 800-room site with its extraordinary patterned stone masonry and many kivas. Next door to Bonito is Kin Kletso, a ruin of a later date, thought to have been built and occupied by immigrants from the northern San Juan region.

Upon seeing these two sites and others—Chetro Ketl, Pueblo del Arroyo, Casa Rinconada—you may wonder what sort of system of manual labor allowed building on such a scale and with such fine stonework. Was the system communal, like the

Petroglyph of Navajo ceremonial figure, Chaco Canyon.

raising of the cathedrals in Europe? Or, like New York City's skyscrapers, were these structures built with excess capital? Imagine, for example, the single task of transporting more than 200,000 logs from distant mountain ranges (see Chimney Rock Pueblo, p. 134) for use as roof beams!

After A.D. 1200, the empty towns of Chaco Canyon deteriorated quietly for centuries. Then, probably in the early 1500s, bands of Apachean peoples began filtering into the Southwest. One of these bands, the Apaches de Nabajo, eventually settled in an area they call the Dinetah (see p. 207) east of Farmington, New Mexico. In the late 1700s, some of these people expanded south into the Chaco country; once again the land of the Chaco Anasazi was being populated, though these newcomers had a totally different way of life from that of the pueblo dwellers.

Navajos still live and work in the Chaco area. In and around the canyon, you can find many Navajo petroglyphs and pictographs from the late 1700s to recent times. And if you hike across the mesas around Chaco Canyon, you are likely to come across the remains of old hogans and sweat lodges that belonged to past generations of Chaco Navajos.

Of the dozen major Chaco Canyon ruins, eight can be reached by road; other sites, such as Penasco Blanco, Tsin Kletsin, and

Pueblo Alto, require some hiking. Still others, while under the park's protection, lie even farther away. Information on reaching these sites is available at the visitor center.

How should you plan a visit to Chaco Canyon? This is really a matter of individual preference. From Farmington or Gallup, you can drive to the park and quickly tour several ruins in half a day. A fuller experience can be had by using available trail guides or taking a ruins tour with a ranger. Consult the visitor center for the daily tour schedule. Staying overnight at the campground to see the canyon early and late in the day and hearing a campfire talk is also worthwhile. Those who especially appreciate the beauty of the canyon and ruins will enjoy staying and hiking at Chaco Canyon for two or more days.

The visitor center has a small museum, toilets, and water fountain, but there are no travel services at Chaco Canyon. Bring your own food, water, and firewoood, and check your gas tank before leaving the main highway. Also, be prepared for hot summer temperatures and cold winds in winter. The nearest restaurants and motels are in the Farmington and Gallup areas.

Suggested reading: *New Light on Chaco Canyon,* edited by David Grant Noble, School of American Research, Santa Fe, New Mexico, 1985.

Village of the Great Kivas

Village of the Great Kivas is on the Zuni Indian Reservation in west-central New Mexico. Zuni Pueblo, about 17 miles from the ruins, is located along New Mexico 53, 35 miles south of Gallup and 71 miles west of Grants. To visit this site, contact the Zuni Tribal Office (505) 782-4481 for permission. Directions to the site can be obtained from the tribal archaeology department at (505) 782-4814.

Unlike the pueblo of Hawikuh, Village of the Great Kivas had long been abandoned when Europeans first entered the American Southwest in 1539, and predates other prehistoric Zuni sites in the region.

The ruins are named for two great kivas that appear as large circular depressions just in front of the pueblo. The presence of two such kivas at such a relatively small site seems unusual, although some explanation may emerge if and when they are fully investigated. Village of the Great Kivas was one of the farthest of Chaco Canyon's outlying communities; in fact, there were several others in the greater Zuni territory between A.D. 1000 and 1150. If you have been to Chaco Canyon, eighty miles to the north, you will recognize aspects of this site, such as the banded

Zuni pictographs, Village of the Great Kivas.

masonry of the great house, as typical Chacoan characteristics. You will also see a resemblance between this site and Casamero (see p. 108), some thirty miles to the northeast.

The pueblo is situated on a slope at the foot of a mesa overlooking Nutria Canyon. Only a few of the site's eighteen rooms are exposed; the rest, however, can be inferred from the existence of substantial earth-covered mounds.

Village of the Great Kivas was excavated in the 1930s by Frank H. H. Roberts, Jr., an archaeologist best known for his research at Shabik'eshchee Village, a large Basketmaker site in Chaco Canyon. He also excavated Chimney Rock Pueblo (see p. 134).

While at Village of the Great Kivas, you will enjoy seeing ancient petroglyphs on rocks behind the site and two panels of pictographs further around the cliff to the right. These paintings, which date to recent decades, represent sacred masks and figures familiar to Zuni ceremonials. Care must be taken not to touch this artwork as it is fragile; several images already have suffered at the hands of vandals.

Village of the Great Kivas is a small, partially excavated, uninterpreted site and will be of less interest to casual tourists than real ruins buffs. It is one more example of the perplexing "Chaco phenomenon," aspects of which have been discussed elsewhere in this book.

Zuni Pueblo, too, especially the historic section with its old mission church (which overlays the prehistoric site of Halona) is a place you may want to visit. Zuni has no motels, but you can purchase gas and groceries, eat at a cafe, and stay at the tribal campground. Other nearby ruins are Hawikuh (see p. 116) and Atsinna Pueblo at El Morro National Monument (see p. 113).

Suggested reading: "Village of the Great Kivas on the Zuni Reservation, New Mexico," by Frank H. H. Roberts, Jr., *Bureau of American Ethnology Bulletin 111*, 1932.

Aztec Ruins National Monument

Aztec Ruins National Monument is located just off U.S. 550 in Aztec, New Mexico, about 14 miles north of Farmington.

We entered the room through the hole in the floor and passed through the open doorway into the northwest room. We broke a hole through the wall and entered the room to the northeast, and there we really did see things! I got into that room and stood, trying my best to take it all in and see everything I could, while that excited crowd were rummaging it, scattering and turning everything into a mess. There were thirteen skeletons ranging from infants to adults. . . .There were several baskets, some of the best that I have ever seen, all well preserved. There were a lot of sandals, some very good, others showing considerable wear. There was a large quantity of pottery, all Mesa Verde. Some of the pottery was very pretty and new looking. There were a great many beads and ornaments . . . [and] turquoise.

I do not know of another person who was in this party of early explorers that is alive now, and the only history or description available is what I remember from childhood.

When we had finished the work, the stuff was taken out and carried off by different members of the party, but where is it now? Nobody knows. . . . I, being only a small kid, did not get my choice of artifacts. I had to take what was left, which made a nice little collection, at that. But it, too, is about all gone.

Sherman S. Howe, 1947

Sealed tombs and buried treasure contain a romance and mystery that inspires both pothunters and archaeologists (who may also have a pothunting demon caged in their souls). Earl H. Morris, who devoted much of his professional life to excavating

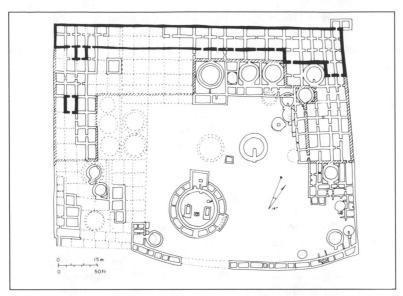

Layout of Aztec Pueblo, which had an estimated 405 rooms and 28 kivas.
Courtesy National Park Service.

and restoring Aztec Ruins, admitted to digging up his first pot at age three and a half: "the clinching event that was to make me an ardent pot hunter, who, later on was to acquire the more creditable, and I hope earned, classification as an archaeologist."

Pothunters and archaeologists, however, are usually in an adversarial relationship, for the success of either one precludes that of the other. Unfortunately, it is the scientist who often arrives on the scene too late. By the time Morris began his investigations at Aztec in 1916 under the auspices of the American Museum of Natural History, parts of the site had been repeatedly looted, its artifacts distributed among homes throughout the area, given away, lost, sold, or destroyed. This large, well-preserved pueblo, however, contained a treasure trove of material, most of which remained beyond the reach of "early explorers" like Sherman Howe. Some sections of the pueblo were three stories (thirty feet) high, and after it was abandoned, the upper story soon slumped onto the second story, thereby sealing off the first floor. In this way, thousands of fragile items were protected from both weather and looters.

Morris's findings quickly led him to the conclusion that Aztec had seen two separate occupations by two different Anasazi groups. His excavations closest to the surface brought to light artifacts of the Mesa Verdean culture with its center to the north. Under this stratum lay a shallow layer of what archaeologists call *sterile fill*—windblown dirt containing no cultural material. This

West wing of Aztec Ruins.

Ceiling in Aztec Ruins.

represented a period of abandonment. But beneath the fill, the excavators found more artifacts, this time bearing the stamp of the Chacoan culture. A prehistoric road that is still discernable today by air connects Aztec to Chaco Canyon, fifty miles to the south.

Morris deduced that Aztec was originally built by Chacoan people, then was abandoned for a period of time, and finally was reoccupied by Mesa Verdeans, who cleaned out and renovated some of the earlier rooms and added some of their own. Tree-ring dates, obtained after Morris had completed his research, confirmed his conclusions: the Chacoan occupation dated to the early 1100s and the Mesa Verdean from about 1225 to 1300.

Some of Morris's findings at Aztec were truly spectacular. One partially burned room in the East Wing contained a rare high-status burial with thousands of oliva shell beads, some mosaic pendants of abalone shell, and a seventy-five-foot necklace containing 40,000 beads. In addition, the room held 200 bushels of unshelled charred corn and a vast amount of pottery vessels and effigies. Thirty-one thousand beads were found in a single container, and at one end of the room lay a pile of 200 quartzite arrow points.

Another rare find was the burial of a "warrior," a six-foot-two-inch man buried with jewelry and wrapped in a turkey-feather blanket. He had with him a large decorated basketry shield, numerous bowls and jars, objects believed to be wooden swords, and other items. Still another Aztec burial was that of a seventeen-year-old girl whose broken forearm had been set with splints before she died, rare evidence of Anasazi medical practices.

Visitors will find the reconstructed West Wing of Aztec Ruins of special interest. Here you may enter a series of rooms that appear in nearly their original condition with walls, ceilings, and architectural details intact. Aztec also is well known for its great kiva, which Morris reconstructed in 1934. The kiva's large interior space is broken only by massive masonry and wood columns that support a roof estimated originally to have weighed over ninety tons. Here, you can easily imagine the elaborate religious rituals of the Anasazi.

Aztec Ruins National Monument has a small museum with good displays of Pueblo artifacts and a short audiovisual program on the natural history and prehistory of the area. Aztec is a large, well-preserved, carefully interpreted, and easily accessible ruin. The entire complex can be viewed superficially in less than an hour, but many visitors may wish to spend more time here. A variety of travel services are located near the monument, and Salmon Ruins (below) is a contemporary site that is only twelve miles away. Some people, after seeing these two Chacoan outliers, will certainly be inspired to visit Chaco Canyon itself.

Suggested reading: *Earl Morris & Southwestern Archaeology*, by Florence C. Lister and Robert H. Lister, University of New Mexico Press, Albuquerque, New Mexico, 1968.

Salmon Ruins

Salmon Ruins are located on the south side of U.S. 64 between Bloomfield and Farmington, New Mexico.

Salmon Ruins were named for Peter Milton Salmon, a Mormon homesteader who settled near the site in 1877. In 1968, the Salmon family, which had safeguarded the ruins for generations, sold it to San Juan County, the citizens of which raised the down payment in a three-day period. Had this support not materialized, the site might have been purchased by a private entrepreneur to be mined for antiquarian souvenirs. Subsequent funds to preserve and study the ruins were contributed by the State of New Mexico, the National Endowment for the Humanities, and other private sources. It is fortunate that these benefactors combined their resources to save this important piece of America's historical heritage.

Salmon is a 300-room pueblo situated on an alluvial terrace above the floodplain of the San Juan River. Excavations conducted in the 1970s by Cynthia Irwin-Williams from Eastern New Mexico

University, with a large crew of archaeologists, students, and volunteers, took place 900 years after the initial building of the pueblo.

A prehistoric road probably linked Salmon Pueblo to Chaco Canyon, fifty miles to the south, and it was Chacoans who first settled here about A.D. 1088. Their basic building materials were quarried sandstone blocks for walls up to thirty-six inches thick, adobe mud for mortar, and timbers to carry the roofs. The trees for the beams were probably felled in the pine forests of southwestern Colorado and floated down the Piedra and San Juan rivers. Laborers from Chimney Rock (see p. 134) may have been involved in this logging operation.

The first inhabitants of Salmon Pueblo stayed scarcely more than two generations. For about a century, the site lay nearly deserted and fell into serious disrepair. Then, between A.D. 1225 and 1240, several hundred Mesa Verdeans reoccupied the pueblo. They renovated many rooms, added several kivas, and stayed for fifty or sixty years before they too left. This sequence of occupation is similar to that of Aztec Pueblo (see p. 127) and other sites in the region, including Kin Kletso within Chaco Canyon. Irwin-Williams commented that "the use of physical space was completely different in the two occupations. The Chacoans required—since they built them that way—large, light, airy, spacious quarters. The secondary occupants . . . did not need such quarters, . . . possibly because they were used to living in smaller houses."

A tragic event occurred at Salmon after A.D. 1263. As archaeologists reconstruct it, a fire broke out in the ceiling of a room and began to spread throughout the surrounding complex. Fifty young children apparently initially escaped the conflagration and were gathered for safety on a nearby kiva roof. When the roof collapsed, the children fell inside, where they later perished in temperatures so hot that the sand on the floor was fused into glass. Prehistoric pueblos, with their wood roofs and compact quarters, were fire traps, and tragedies such as Salmon's were not uncommon.

When you walk about Salmon, consider the amount of labor and the degree of architectural planning and engineering skills required to build the pueblo—the same is true of nearby Aztec Pueblo and the even larger towns of Chaco Canyon. You will certainly agree that this was an extremely energetic and well-organized society during its florescence. For an agricultural people, however, no amount of social and political organization or military might can long endure a shortage of rainfall. Farmers are subject to the unpredictable whims of nature, and when environmental factors shift, people suffer. This may explain the ultimate abandonment of Salmon Pueblo in the late 1200s. On

Salmon Pueblo.

Chaco Masonry at Salmon Ruins.

the other hand, future archaeologists may uncover other reasons why these Puebloans left their idyllic riverine home.

Visitors can walk around the ruins on a self-guiding interpretive trail, which initially passes by the rustic Salmon family homestead, then meanders through the pueblo. One impressive feature to see within the apartment complex is a tower kiva built on a twenty-foot-high platform of specially selected rock.

The San Juan County Museum Association manages the ruins and maintains a museum and research library overlooking the ruins. The site and museum are open to the public daily at a nominal fee. Museum displays include beautifully crafted prehistoric Indian tools and utensils and fine ceramics. In addition, an interesting slide presentation on the archaeological excavations is offered.

Travel services of all kinds are available in nearby Farmington and Bloomfield. Visits to Salmon Ruins and Aztec National Monument can easily be combined in the same day.

> Suggested reading: *The Chacoan Prehistory of the San Juan Basin,* by R. Gwinn Vivian, Academic Press, San Diego, California, 1990.

Chimney Rock Archaeological Area

Chimney Rock is located approximately 20 miles west of Pagosa Springs, Colorado, on Colorado 151, 3 miles south of U.S. 160. From 15 May to 15 September, National Forest Service staff conduct daily guided tours of the ruins. The tours begin at 9 A.M. at the well-marked forest service gate on the west side of the road and take about 2.5 hours. Reservations are needed for groups of 7 or more people; call (303) 264-2268 or contact the Pagosa Springs Ranger District, San Juan National Forest, P.O. Box 310, Pagosa Springs, CO 81147.

Chimney Rock is one of the more spectacular ruins in the Southwest. The rock spire for which the site is named is thrust up above the surrounding landscape and has served as a landmark for Indians, pioneers, trappers, and travelers. Archaeologists have found hundreds of Anasazi sites, including sizable pueblos in this general area, among which Chimney Rock Pueblo is the best known. This site and several others have been excavated, stabilized, and interpreted for the public.

The Anasazi Indians (ancestors of the present-day Pueblo Indians) first settled the Chimney Rock area about A.D. 925. These early settlers were culturally affiliated with the Mesa Verdeans to the west, as evidenced by their styles of pottery and architecture. The majority lived in small communities usually situated on terraces overlooking the Piedra River Valley where they cultivated corn and beans. Others, like the Chimney Rock Pueblo inhabitants who arrived later, lived high up on the mesa, where today's tours are conducted. Still other Anasazi chose to make their homes in smaller hamlets, isolated dwellings, and seasonal campsites close to ravines in which they cultivated floodwater garden plots.

The Chimney Rock Anasazi lived much the same as their contemporaries elsewhere: To subsist, they generally combined farming with gathering plants and seeds and hunting game, as well as trading with neighbors. But what is remarkable about the Chimney Rock folks is their apparent ability to cope with high-altitude living, where the growing season for corn was precariously short and winters bitterly cold. On the other hand, game seems to have been abundant, and the Chimney Rock Anasazi successfully hunted deer, elk, mountain sheep, porcupine, rabbits, and small rodents.

The real highlight of a visit here is Chimney Rock Pueblo itself, sometimes referred to as the Great House. It is situated on a narrow mesa, at an elevation of 7,600 feet, very close to the Chimney Rock. The mesa is so narrow, in fact, that sheer cliffs drop precipitously off on both sides, and because of erosion, parts of room walls even have tumbled down into the valley below. The two-story Chacoan outlier has an estimated fifty-five rooms including two kivas. It was not a remarkably large site, but it efficiently took advantage of the very limited building space available on the ridge. Its kivas, well-conceived general plan, and "core and veneer" walls that are neatly built with layered and chinked

sandstone blocks all show the engineering and design skills of Chaco Canyon craftsmanship. You do not need to be a scientist to recognize that this pueblo was built by an inspired, powerful, well-organized, and highly motivated people.

So what happened here? What can we surmise about the history of the Chimney Rock people? We know that the first Mesa Verdean settlers arrived about A.D. 925 to begin a viable farming life in the valleys. Over the years, their population increased, and their hamlets grew in numbers. Then, around 1076, when the Chacoan empire was expanding (Chaco Canyon is ninety-three miles to the southwest), a group of Chacoans apparently migrated to Chimney Rock and established a settlement. They selected, perhaps symbolically, the highest, most dominant building site available and built the majority of the pueblo in the early 1090s. Why choose a bare rock outcropping a thousand feet above water as a house site when baskets of corn had to be lugged up the tortuous trail from the distant terraces below and ceramic pots of water had to hauled up an exhausting ascent in order to mix building mortar and to provide drinking water?

One explanation that comes to mind—not unique in human history—is that the Chacoans were a ruling elite who coerced more docile peasant folk to work for them. Perhaps religious fervor rather than coercion was the motivation. All evidence shows that between A.D. 1030 and 1140 the Chacoans had a wide-spread sphere of influence. Many books have been written about this, most recently *The Chacoan Prehistory of the San Juan Basin*, by R. Gwinn Vivian (see p. 134). What is more, the people of Chimney Rock may have had something the Chacoans needed—lumber. Chaco Canyon was virtually treeless, and yet, its dozen or more great towns consumed more than 200,000 logs as roof supports. Where did this lumber come from? One place may have been the forests around Chimney Rock. Chimney Rock's elevation, while hindering corn production, may have been an advantage to a timber industry. The process of felling a large tree probably took three years. First, the trunk was girdled. Then, after the tree had died and cured, it was laboriously chopped down using a stone axe. After being felled, trees may have been skidded down the snowy slopes to the Piedra River during the winter and floated downstream to some processing point more accessible to Chaco Canyon. The San Juan, in fact, flows right past Salmon Pueblo (see p. 131), a major outlier linked to Chaco by a major prehistoric road.

Of course, the lumber connection is only a theory. Archaeology abounds in theories, many of which, while appearing plausible,

---

View of Chimney Rock and Companion Rock from the ruins.

Chimney Rock Pueblo.

are hard to prove. Perhaps one day, some enterprising person will find caches of prehistoric axes, draw knives, and rasps used to process the giant ponderosa logs that ended up at Chaco Canyon.

There are other interesting theories relating to Chimney Rock. The Taos Indians of northern New Mexico, for example, believe Chimney Rock to have been an ancestral Taos shrine. The sacred nature of the shrine may have been based on its association with the spire that personified the Pueblo Twin War Gods. This line of thinking may partially explain the existence of the site or, at least, its placement.

Recently, archaeoastronomers, who are looking for possible relationships between archaeological sites and celestial bodies, have discovered an unusual occurrence called a "lunar standstill," which happens every eighteen years. On these occasions, the moon appears to stand still between Chimney Rock and an adja-cent rock spire. Other astronomical observations also are being studied. Perhaps, 900 years ago, this was an observatory that played a part in Anasazi religious rituals.

To proceed to less speculative topics, visitors to Chimney Rock follow their guide by car several miles up into the San Juan foothills to an upper parking area where the walking tour starts. A gentle, paved trail leads to several small ruins, including an excavated great kiva, a small kiva with several contingent rooms, and a strange circular hole beautifully hand-carved into the bed-rock. This unusual feature perplexes archaeologists, though some, for lack of a better term, refer to it as an exterior *sipapu*. A *sipapu* is a small hole in the floor of a kiva that leads symbolically to the underworld.

You then walk to three adjacent, large, excavated, circular rooms that, while resembling kivas, are described by the experts as residences. From here, you climb a fairly steep unpaved trail to the mesa top, passing the "guardhouse" along the way, a site with a series of rooms and kivas perched literally on the cliff's edge. Finally, after a 500-foot ascent, you arrive at the literal and figura-tive highpoint of the entire tour—Chimney Rock Pueblo. This site is truly impressive for its fine Chacoan architecture as well as its captivating view over the countryside, including Chimney Rock and another spire, Companion Rock. The site has two kivas contained in a block of rooms. Just beyond it, a modern fire tower offers an even better perspective.

Archaeological studies at Chimney Rock began in 1921–1922 with surveys and excavations by J. A. Jeancon and Frank H. H. Roberts, Jr., sponsored jointly by the Colorado State Historical Society and the Natural History Society of Colorado in cooperation with the University of Denver. Investigations along the San Juan River (now Navajo Reservoir) were carried out in the late 1950s and early 1960s by the Museum of New Mexico, and between 1970 and 1972, more work was done in the Chimney Rock District by Frank W. Eddy of the University of Colorado. Eddy identified ninety-one sites, of which he excavated four to prepare for public tours.

In summary, Chimney Rock is well worth seeing and the tour and hike are enjoyable. Even though the tour is only about two hours long, a canteen of water is recommended, as are field glasses.

Accommodations and travel services are readily available in nearby Pagosa Springs and Durango.

Suggested reading: *The Outlier Survey*, by Robert P. Powers et al., Division of Cultural Research, National Park Service, Albuquerque, New Mexico, 1983. *Archaeological Investigations at Chimney Rock Mesa: 1970–1972*, by Frank W. Eddy, The Colorado Archaeological Society, Boulder, Colorado, 1977.

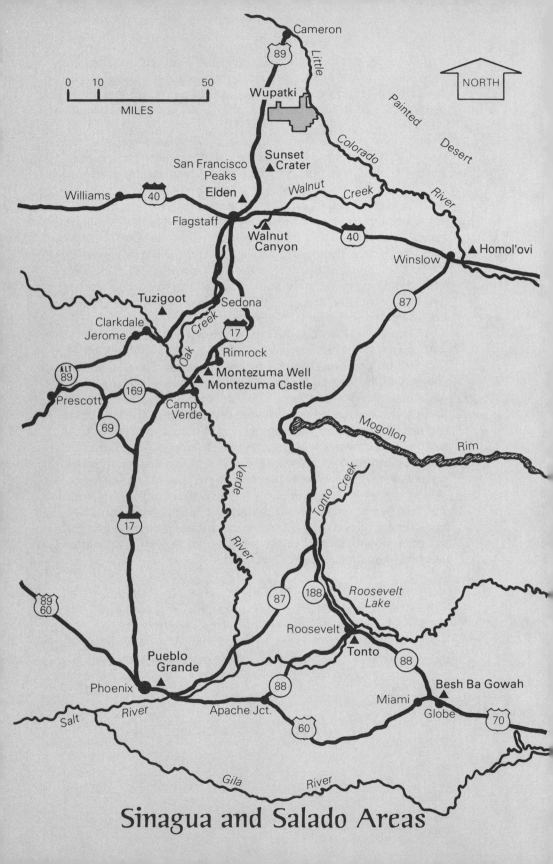

Sinagua and Salado Areas

THE SINAGUA AND THE SALADO
People in Between

The Sinagua and the Salado are two relatively obscure southwestern peoples who lived prehistorically in central and northern Arizona. Both cultures were heavily influenced by such dominant neighbors as the Anasazi and Hohokam; eventually, both groups blended with their neighbors to such an extent that they disappeared from the archaeological record as distinct groups.

The Sinagua

Despite their name, which means "without water" in Spanish, the Sinagua (seen-awa) did have water and were successful farmers in the region between the San Francisco Peaks near present-day Flagstaff, Arizona, and the Verde Valley to the south. The earliest northern Sinagua sites date from about A.D. 675 and consist of pithouse villages in areas where the piñon-juniper uplands meet the higher-elevation ponderosa forests. The Indians used both zones for hunting and gathering and raised crops in the fertile alluvial soils of basins along the flanks of the mountains. Initially small in population, their numbers increased, and by A.D. 900, they had established trading relationships with Kayenta Anasazi people to the north and Hohokam to the south. Their farming methods also became more elaborate as evidenced today by the remains of terraces and field houses.

The southern Sinagua farmed the fertile mesas along the Mogollon Rim, using rocks as a garden mulch to moderate soil temperatures and lengthen growing seasons. They also had constant contact with Hohokam settlers and traders from the south, with whom they exchanged goods and from whom they learned irrigation technology. Ball courts, a hallmark of Hohokam culture, are found in both the Verde Valley and Flagstaff areas, further indicating the close ties between the Sinagua and Hohokam.

Travelers approaching Flagstaff today from the north or east will notice the presence of a number of cinder cones. In 1064, a series of volcanic eruptions began that resulted in the formation of Sunset Crater and the spread of an estimated half a billion tons of cinders and ash over some 800 square miles. These fantastic natural events must have profoundly affected the local residents. The eruptions continued off and on for 200 years, producing ash, cinders, and lava flows. Today, one can take a fascinating geological walking tour in Sunset Crater National Monument to see the effects of these eruptions.

A former generation of archaeological scholars explained the post-eruption flowering of Sinagua culture by describing a "land-rush" scenario. According to their theory, prehistoric peoples from surrounding regions poured into the northern Sinagua lands to take advantage of agricultural conditions suddenly enhanced by the newly formed cover of ash and cinder, which fertilized the soils and created a moisture-conserving mulch. They believed that Anasazi, Cohonina, Hohokam, and Cibola people immigrated to the Sunset Crater region to live side by side with the native Sinaguans. The subsequent peaceful intermingling of cultures resulted in exchanges of ideas and practices at many levels, including religion, social organization, building techniques, and crafts. In the process, the Sinagua learned pueblo-style architecture and irrigation farming and developed new, more sophisticated cultural forms. The Wupatki National Monument area (see p. 148) was supposedly the center of this unprecedented cultural blending.

Some current researchers, however, question the land-rush model. They point out that it takes a long time for the nutrients in volcanic ash and cinders to break down and enrich the soil, and since pre-1064 sites were buried by the eruptions, there is no basis upon which to compare post-eruption population estimates. What is more, the existence of a large number of post-eruption sites may only reflect a small population moving around more. The immigration theory, too, has been challenged, for it now is clear that the Anasazi and Kayenta ceramics found at Sinagua sites were imported rather than locally made by immigrants.

Peter J. Pilles, Jr., and other present researchers believe that factors in addition to volcanic eruptions also influenced Sinagua cultural development. The century following A.D. 1064, for example, was marked by increased rainfall, in response to which the northern Sinagua may have moved to lower elevations such as

Imported pottery excavated at Elden Pueblo.

the Wupatki National Monument area.

Beginning about A.D. 1150, the northern Sinagua began to reach their highest cultural expression (Elden Phase), which is apparent in technological achievements, more complex social organization, and population growth. Between A.D. 1150 and 1250, large villages, such as Elden Pueblo (see p. 146) and Ridge Ruin, were established, and Sinagua settlements spread into the Wupatki and Walnut Canyon areas and as far away as the Mogollon Rim. The discovery of the "Magician's Burial" at Ridge Ruin offers a clue to the social stratification that had evolved. The so-called magician was clearly a high-status individual—he was buried with over 600 objects, including pottery, baskets, jewelry, and many other items of ritual significance. Hopi Indians who have studied these burial goods recognize this person as a high-ranking member of their *Motswimi* or Warrior Society. Their perspective, which is reinforced by archaeological data, points to the Sinagua ancestry of some Hopi clans.

Developments among the southern Sinagua paralleled those of the Flagstaff area during this period. Construction of Tuzigoot, Montezuma Castle, and numerous cliff dwellings near present-day Sedona, Arizona, were initiated in the mid-1200s. The Sinagua also began to build "forts" overlooking canyons in the uplands. While these sites suggest the presence of an external threat, no evidence of warfare has been found, and some scholars think they may have been trading outposts or distribution centers. After A.D. 1300, southern Sinagua population concentrated in large, highly visible sites, such as Tuzigoot (see p. 155) and Montezuma Castle (see p. 158), that dominated smaller surrounding satellite pueblos.

The northern Sinagua left many of their villages in the San Francisco Peaks area in the late 1200s and 1300s to move northeast

Wupatki Pueblo.

to the Wupatki area and to sites such as Nuvakwewtaqa on Anderson Mesa to the southeast. In the early 1400s, the southern Sinagua abandoned the Verde Valley, also migrating toward Nuvakwewtaqa and the Hopi country. At this point, Sinagua culture begins to blend with that of the Hopi, who view these late Sinagua sites as ancestral. Sunset Crater, in fact, is the home of Yaponcha, the Hopi wind god, and the San Francisco Peaks are where the Hopi kachinas reside during a large part of the year. Even Elden Pueblo is the subject of a Hopi legend.

Archaeology still has much to contribute to our understanding of the Sinagua. Their complex story, which involves settlement in contrasting environments and contacts with strong outside cultures, is one that has stimulated differing views among archaeologists over the years. The next chapter in this evolving field of research promises to be exciting.

The Salado

Like the Sinagua, the Salado Indians developed a culture that blended Anasazi, Hohokam, and Mogollon traits. Originating along the Little Colorado River in north-central Arizona, Salado culture expanded south to the headwaters of the Gila and Salt (*salado* is Spanish for "salt") rivers. The Salado people lived in the Tonto Basin and Globe-Miami area between roughly A.D. 1100 and 1450.

It was the legendary explorer-anthropologist Adolph F. Bandelier who first detected Salado cutural attributes when he was investigating ruins around Globe in 1883. He was followed in the 1920s by Erich F. Schmidt from the American Museum of Natural History. Schmidt excavated numerous sites and created a significant Salado database. Also in the 1920s, Harold and Winifred Gladwin established a major research center known as Gila Pueblo in Globe, which focused on Salado studies.

Archaeologists differ on how to define Salado culture and what its origins were. Some researchers believe an actual migration of people came into the Tonto Basin from elsewhere, while others espouse the view that Salado culture was formed by a spread of ideas and practices among indigenous folk.

Clearly, Hohokam people lived in the Tonto Basin and the Globe-Miami area prior to the Salado, and they were probably instrumental in teaching the Salado irrigation farming and certain craft arts. The Salado, on the other hand, likely introduced the concept of above-ground masonry building, learned from the Anasazi. They also had a distinctive and beautiful form of pottery—Gila Polychrome—which is noted for its black and white designs on a red base and was produced between the late thirteenth and early fifteenth centuries. Most other Salado traits in the archaeological record closely resemble those of their Hohokam and Anasazi neighbors.

Salado culture disappeared in the early 1400s, when it was either absorbed by other groups or underwent such internal modifications that its descendants are not identifiable as Salado. Traces of Gila Polychrome ceramics dating to about A.D. 1450 have been found to the east and south, suggesting a possible absorption into Mogollon-derived communities in southern New Mexico.

Roosevelt Dam, constructed in 1911, flooded the Tonto Basin, forming Roosevelt Lake and inundating the majority of Salado archaeological sites. Since the science of archaeology was in its infancy at this time, many questions concerning this prehistoric group remain unanswered. Salado sites that are open to the public are the ruins of Tonto National Monument (see p. 163) and the pueblo of Besh Ba Gowah (see p. 165) in Globe, Arizona.

Suggested reading: "The 1976 Salado Conference," edited by David E. Doyel and Emil W. Haury, *The Kiva*, vol. 42, no. 1, The Arizona Archaeological and Historical Society, Tucson, Arizona, 1976.

Elden Pueblo

Elden Pueblo is located on the west side of U.S. 89, 1.5 miles north of its interchange with Interstate 40, in Flagstaff, Arizona.

Ancient ruins have traditionally been excavated by two groups—archaeologists and looters. In too many instances, the archaeological findings have been reported only in scholarly journals that are, for all practical purposes, beyond the reach of the general public. As for pothunters, the rewards of their activities are usually hidden away or sold to collectors with no public educational benefit.

At Elden Pueblo, an important Sinagua site on the outskirts of Flagstaff, a new type of "public archaeology" is being explored in which people interested in the past actively participate in the archaeological process. These amateurs range from grade school to university students and from Flagstaff residents to Elderhostel groups. The program has helped to dispel the exclusivity of traditional archaeology and initiate a broad spectrum of people into the value and fascination of investigating past cultures. It also

Life at Elden Pueblo. Illustration by Brian Donahue. Courtesy Coconino National Forest.

has contributed to the transformation of Elden Pueblo from a group of half-forgotten mounds to an educational public monument. Elden Pueblo's public program has been developed and administered by Coconino National Forest archaeologists with support from other organizations.

The pueblo, which has between sixty and seventy rooms, thrived between about A.D. 1100 and 1250 in a shady ponderosa forest at the base of Mt. Elden. Rocks eroded from the mountain provided building stones used by Elden's residents, and a spring on its slopes offered at least one permanent water source. Only a few miles to the northeast is Sunset Crater, whose eruptions, beginning in A.D. 1064, transformed the environment of the Flagstaff area. The inhabitants of Elden were able to collect plant foods and other resources from varied environmental zones; plant crops in alluvial parks within half a mile of home; and hunt game, including elk, deer, antelope, mountain sheep, bear, coyote, squirrel, gopher, rabbit, and turkey.

The Elden site contains a "community room" that measures thirty by thirty-six feet, about four times larger than the typical residential and storage rooms in the pueblo. This room is encircled by a bench and was provided fresh air by means of a slab-lined ventilator shaft. Many thick layers of mud plaster cover the floor. Probably, it was used as a meeting place for all the pueblo's residents. The ruin has other interesting features. It is surrounded on at least three sides by a unique formalized activity area with plastered surfaces and storage and roasting pits, and it has three cemeteries lying just outside the main apartment complex.

All indications are that Elden Pueblo was a significant regional center in the twelfth and thirteenth centuries. In addition to farmers, it had craft specialists and some residents of high social rank that was probably hereditary. The Hopi Indians, who call the site *Pasiwvi*, "place of coming together," view Elden as an ancestral village and the former home of members of their Snake, Water, Badger, Antelope, and other clans. As recently as the 1930s, Hopis stopped at the site to pray while traveling to the San Francisco Peaks, their sacred mountains. Hopi oral history regarding Elden Pueblo reinforces archaeologists' views that the Sinagua people played a role in the development of Hopi culture.

Elden was partially excavated in 1926 by Jesse Walter Fewkes and John Peabody Harrington of the Smithsonian Institution. The ruins were the first major site in the Flagstaff area to be scientifically investigated. In 1966–1968, Roger E. Kelly directed a Northern Arizona University field school at the site. Despite this past research and the encroachment of urban development into the site, Elden still holds promise for future archaeological study.

Other nearby archaeological ruins include Wupatki (see p.148) and Walnut Canyon (see p. 153) national monuments. In addition, Sunset Crater and the Museum of Northern Arizona are well worth visiting.

Suggested reading: "The Destruction of Elden Pueblo: A Hopi Story," by Edmund Nequatewa, Plateau 28(2), Museum of Northern Arizona, Flagstaff, Arizona, 1955.

Wupatki National Monument

Wupatki National Monument is 14 miles east of Arizona 89 between Flagstaff and Cameron. A 36-mile driving loop from Arizona 89 passes through this monument and Sunset Crater National Monument.

Wupatki National Monument, where the ruins of Wupatki, Wukoki, Citadel, Lomaki, and other sites are found, holds one of the most spacious and desolate panoramas in the Southwest. In the extreme, temperatures can plummet to zero in winter and over 110 degrees in summer. Only the hardiest vegetation is able to grow in this region where scant rains often evaporate quickly in the dry heat and sweeping winds. Wupatki seems a most unlikely locale to have nurtured a human population that once reached several thousand people.

The finding of an 11,000-year-old Clovis spearpoint suggests that some of the Southwest's first human residents roamed through the Wupatki area. Along the gravel terraces of the Little Colorado River, archaeologists also have found stone tool manufacturing sites used by Archaic people prior to A.D. 500.

Today, the cinders deposited by the eruptions of Sunset Crater that began in A.D. 1064 are still very much in evidence. However, they buried pre-eruption archaeological sites, making it difficult to estimate the area's early population. Although the layer of ash and cinder from the volcano certainly benefited farming by creating a mulch to conserve ground moisture, population growth at Wupatki in the 1100s probably is more a result of an increase in rainfall in the twelfth century. The densest concentration of people was on Antelope Prairie in the western sector of the monument. In this higher-elevation area, native farmers took advantage of more precipitation and better soils to cultivate their crops. They built check dams to direct water flow to their garden plots, larger dams in natural catchments, and single-room field houses for shelter when they were tending their crops.

An extensive archaeological survey of the monument conducted in the 1980s under the direction of Bruce A. Anderson revealed

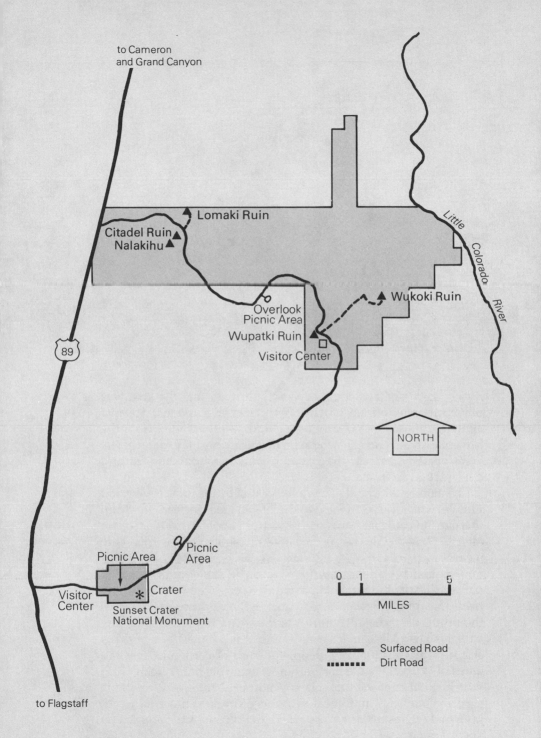

to Cameron
and Grand Canyon

Lomaki Ruin

Citadel Ruin
Nalakihu

89

Overlook
Picnic Area

Wukoki Ruin

Wupatki Ruin

Visitor Center

NORTH

Little
Colorado

River

Picnic Area

Picnic
Area

Visitor
Center

Crater

Sunset Crater
National Monument

to Flagstaff

0   1   5

MILES

————— Surfaced Road
••••••••• Dirt Road

Wupatki National Monument

Wukoki Pueblo, Wupatki National Monument.

nearly 3,000 archaeological sites and showed that the area was inhabited prehistorically by a mix of cultures. In addition to Sinagua artifacts, the survey collections include pottery traded from the Kayenta Anasazi people, whose main culture area lay to the north; Winslow Anasazi from the east; Cohonina folk from the west; and Prescott people from the south.

The monument's headquarters are located by the ruins of Wupatki Pueblo, which was excavated in the 1930s. Tree-ring samples from this site indicate that it was occupied from about A.D. 1106 to soon after 1212 by the Sinagua people. Interesting items recovered here include pieces of turquoise and shell jewelry, copper bells, numerous textiles and baskets, cotton fiber, and the skeleton of a buried parrot. Clearly, the Wupatki people were engaged in far-reaching trade. Near the pueblo is a ball court, which further underscores the influence of distant cultures to the south upon this area. The ball game had Mesoamerican roots and was adopted, and perhaps adapted, by the Hohokam people of southern Arizona. The ball court at Wupatki is the northernmost example of this feature, in which ritual contests took place. Another feature at Wupatki is a large circular "amphitheater," whose original function is not known. Perhaps it was a place where the community gathered on special occasions.

The Kayenta Anasazi ruins of Wukoki, Citadel, and Lomaki can easily be visited by taking the driving loop through the monument.

Petroglyphs at Wupatki National Monument.

Other more distant sites also may be reached with special permission from the Park Service. There are also many Anasazi petroglyphs on the flat-surfaced basaltic rocks of the area, especially in the vicinity of the Crack-in-Rock ruins. A few examples of Hopi rock art are to be found, some denoting known Hopi clans. The petroglyphs depict humans playing flutes, hunting, and giving birth; a variety of animals, birds, and insects; and many graphic designs, including large spirals, which Hopi and Zuni Indians believe to represent migrations. Polly Schaafsma, a noted rock art scholar, has related the Wupatki petroglyph designs to similar motifs found on regional pottery and textiles. This relationship opens up another method of dating petroglyphs and offers new insights into the cultural affiliations of the Sinagua people. Some petroglyphs duplicate patterns found on textiles that were made between A.D. 1100 and 1300; others resemble designs found on Flagstaff black-on-white and Wupatki black-on-white ceramic vessels, which date from A.D. 1100 to 1225.

The historical period at Wupatki has witnessed an interesting series of developments. The story of Mormon settlers, Anglo

Sunset Crater.

cattle ranchers, Navajo sheepherders, miners, traders, and rail-road people would fill an·entire book. One Navajo family, the descendents of Peshlakai Etsidi who moved here in 1870, still lives within the monument boundaries.

The Wupatki visitor center includes a small informative exhibition on the region's history and prehistory. Although picnic sites are available, the area's frequent blustery winds often discourage sitting outdoors. Visitors should also plan to see Sunset Crater just to the south of Wupatki and take the interpretive trail through the lava flow. Sunset Crater National Monument also has a campground in the woods that is open from spring through fall. Travel services can be found along Route 89, especially near Flagstaff and Cameron. Less than an hour's drive south is Walnut Canyon National Monument (opposite), another center of Sinagua life in a much different natural setting.

Suggested reading: *Of Men and Volcanoes: The Sinagua of Northern Arizona,* by Albert H. Schroeder, Southwestern Monuments Association, Globe, Arizona, 1977.

Cliff dwelling in Walnut Canyon.

Walnut Canyon National Monument

Walnut Canyon National Monument is 3 miles from the Walnut Canyon exit on Interstate 40, 7 miles east of Flagstaff, Arizona.

Ruins aside, to see Walnut Canyon is a memorable experience, for the canyon is a natural haven sheltered from the outside world by 400-foot cliffs. The canyon is full of cliff dwellings, which are a bonus to its stunning scenery.

Like Wupatki and the Verde Valley, Walnut Canyon was a center of Sinagua culture. The Sinagua Indians took advantage of cave-like niches along the canyon walls in which they built houses of limestone slabs and mud mortar. These are not the village-sized cliff dwellings of Mesa Verde; rather, they are cozy extended-family dwellings scattered within earshot of each other throughout the area. Less visible are pueblos with small outlying field houses on the canyon rims, where more people may have lived. Some of the pueblos are associated with "forts," which are quite inaccessible, situated just below the rims. These forts, like those of Hovenweep, perplex archaeologists, who have speculated wildly on their purpose.

Only one site in the canyon dates as early as A.D. 800 or 900, and none dates to between 900 and 1100. Sinagua people lived in the general vicinity during these centuries but apparently shunned Walnut Canyon itself. Between A.D. 1150 and 1225, however, the canyon and mesa tops must have hummed with the activities of the many families living there. The canyon offered sheltering caves, water sources, many native plants to be harvested, and plentiful game. The open lands outside the canyon contained suitable areas for farming.

The Sinagua left Walnut Canyon after 1225, probably for the same reasons that they also left Wupatki. Some families may have drifted south to the Verde Valley, perhaps to join relatives at Montezuma Castle (see p. 158), Tuzigoot (see p. 155), and other pueblos. Or they may have traveled east toward present-day Winslow and the Hopi country.

European-Americans did not enter this region in sizable numbers until the latter part of the nineteenth century when they made recreational outings to Walnut Canyon. By the early 1880s, this was a favorite place for treasure hunting and pothunting. To facilitate digging in dark inner rooms, some looters went so far as to dynamite outer walls. Needless to say, before long these activities took a heavy toll on the condition of the cliff dwellings.

By the early 1900s, civic leaders in the town of Flagstaff realized that they were fast losing an important potential tourist attraction and moved to establish some protection for the ruins. But in 1915, when Woodrow Wilson declared Walnut Canyon a national monument, only a single ranger was stationed at the monument to control visitors. Eighteen years later, supervision tightened when the monument was turned over to the National Park Service. By 1942, with the help of the Civilian Conservation Corps, the ruins had been stabilized, many trail improvements had been completed, and guides were assigned to accompany most visitor groups.

Walnut Canyon's cliff dwellings had been so devastated by looters over the years that one archaeologist referred to the place as "a monument to vandalism." But cliff dwellings, which had absorbed the brunt of the damages, were only one dimension of the canyon's archaeology; virtually untouched were other types of sites, especially on the rims, and archaeologists have found much to study in them. The first of these was Dr. Harold S. Colton, a zoology professor at the University of Pennsylvania. After Colton's initial visit to the canyon in 1912, he returned annually to study the ruins and survey the canyon. In 1926, he moved to Flagstaff with his family and founded the Museum of Northern Arizona. Colton was soon joined by Lyndon Hargrave, and together, they conducted the first professional excavation in the canyon. Archaeological research has continued sporadically over the decades. A complete national monument survey in the 1980s identified 242 sites ranging from small artifact scatters to cliff dwellings to multiroomed pueblos.

Walnut Canyon has a visitor center with interpretive exhibits on the canyon's natural and human history. From the center, a mile-long trail, which is scenic but steep, loops through the canyon. The trail passes by several cliff houses and has views of many others. Field glasses are recommended.

Flagstaff offers a variety of all tourist facilities and is a good center from which to visit not only Walnut Canyon but Wupatki (see p. 148), Sunset Crater, the Museum of Northern Arizona, Oak Creek Canyon, and even the South Rim of the Grand Canyon.

Suggested reading: "Walnut Canyon: A View into the Past," by Pat H. Stein and Anne R. Baldwin, in *Wupatki and Walnut Canyon*, Ancient City Press, Santa Fe, New Mexico, 1993.

Tuzigoot National Monument

Tuzigoot National Monument is located along U.S. 89A, between Cottonwood and Clarkdale, Arizona.

The marked dissimilarity of Arizona's Sinagua monuments—Wupatki, Elden, Walnut Canyon, Montezuma Castle, and Tuzigoot—offers insight into the very nature of Sinagua culture. Wupatki (see p. 148) appears as a tall isolated castle in the open desert; Elden's (see p. 146) mounds lie in the woods of Flagstaff suburbs; Walnut Canyon (see p. 153) contains a multitude of small dispersed cliff houses; Montezuma Castle (see p. 158) stands as a large, concentrated, defensive cliff dwelling; and Tuzigoot (see p. 155) is a hill town. The differing characteristics of these sites reflect the adaptiveness of Sinagua culture.

The Verde Valley was an ideal area for settlement, endowed as it was, and is, with a warm climate, fertile soils, and good water

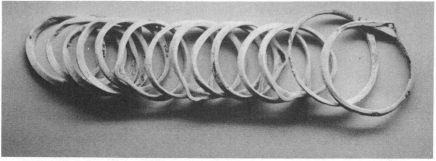

Shell bracelets, Tuzigoot Museum.

Tuzigoot and the Verde Valley.

sources. Archaeologists first recognize Sinagua culture about
A.D. 700 with the appearance of pithouses, agriculture, and pottery.
About the same time, Hohokam people migrated up here from
the Salt River Valley around present-day Phoenix, bringing with
them a developing expertise in irrigation farming and crafts. In addition, some Kayenta Anasazi appear to have settled in the valley.

Tuzigoot is situated on a 120-foot limestone ridge overlooking
the Verde River and Valley. A few dwellings may have existed
here prior to A.D. 1000, and more were added in the early 1100s.
The real growth of the pueblo, however, took place in the mid-
1200s, when many Sinagua moved here, possibly from the environs of present-day Flagstaff. At this time, when the population
of the northern Sinagua area was dramatically decreasing, the
Verde Valley's population concentrated in large fortified pueblos
close to the river. Tuzigoot's population probably reached a peak
of about 225 people, who lived by farming, hunting and gather-

ing, and trading. They were well situated strategically to carry out the latter with the Anasazi and Hohokam, as well as with Mogollon groups to the east. Coveted resources over which the Verde Valley residents had control included mineral deposits, salt, and cotton, and among their imports were shells from the Gulf of California and parrots from locations far to the south.

The first Europeans to see Tuzigoot were probably members of the Antonio Espejo exploratory expedition in 1583. Three hundred years later, mining operations were initiated in Jerome, where copper had been quarried by Indians since prehistoric times. Even today, mining operations border the Tuzigoot ruins. In 1932, federal relief funds were made available to conduct two years of archaeological investigations at the pueblo. In a relatively short period, the ruins were almost entirely excavated by a large force of laborers under the direction of two University of Arizona graduate students, Louis Caywood and Edward H. Spicer. Archaeology in this era did not have the scientific basis that it does today, and as a result, much data about Tuzigoot's past were not recorded, and little material was left for future research. This information gap will eventually be filled when other contemporary sites in the valley are excavated using modern methods.

Tuzigoot's visitor center has a very fine exhibit of archaeological material, including jewelry, basketry, tools, textiles, religious objects, and an interesting room reconstruction. Visitors should plan about half an hour to see the museum and the same amount of time to tour the ruins. The trail is easy to negotiate and has a sweeping view of the Verde Valley.

Tuzigoot is located between Flagstaff and Prescott and travelers will enjoy seeing the beautiful scenery of Oak Creek Canyon and Sedona to the north and the historic mining town of Jerome to the south. Any itinerary in this area should also include Montezuma Castle (see p. 158), which is twenty-seven miles to the east.

Suggested reading: *Tuzigoot: An Archaeological Overview,* by Dana Hartman, Museum of Northern Arizona, Flagstaff, Arizona, 1976. *People of the Verde Valley,* edited by Stephen Trimble, Museum of Northern Arizona, Flagstaff, Arizona, 1981.

Montezuma Castle National Monument

Montezuma Castle National Monument in northern Arizona is located several miles east of Interstate 17, just north of Camp Verde and less than an hour's drive south of Flagstaff. The exit from Interstate 17 is well marked.

Montezuma, the sixteenth-century Aztec ruler, was never exiled to northern Arizona, but had such a fate befallen him, no more fitting domicile could he have had than the "castle" that today bears his name. Impregnably situated on the ledges of a sheer cliff overlooking Beaver Creek in the lush Verde Valley, Montezuma Castle is a striking example of prehistoric Indian architecture. Its seventeen rooms reach up to five stories. The excellent condition of the pueblo can be attributed to a provision that forbids visitors from rambling through the rooms. Occupied 600 and more years ago, the pueblo represents one of the last sites of the Sinagua Indians.

Scholars have long argued over both the origins and fate of the Sinagua who lived in and around this area. A farming people, they were in the Verde Valley as early as A.D. 700, thriving not only on the valley's rich agricultural properties, but also on the diversity of resources in the nearby uplands. Archaeological evidence shows that they traded with surrounding tribes, such as the Anasazi to the north and east and the Hohokam, whose heartland was to the south.

Hohokam culture (see p. 15) centered in the area around present-day Phoenix, but the influence of these expert farmers spread north into the Verde Valley and even as far as the Flagstaff area. The Sinagua and Hohokam seem to have coexisted in the Verde Valley, sharing their respective talents and knowledge.

The Verde Valley, then as today, was warm, fertile, and well watered. The Verde River and its tributaries, such as Beaver Creek, were used to irrigate crops in the bottomlands. It was logical for people to be attracted to this area, especially when conditions deteriorated elsewhere. In the early 1100s, the valley's population increased and consolidated, and around that time, the Sinagua built the first few rooms of the Montezuma cliff dwelling. The eruptions of Sunset Crater to the north, which began in 1064, may have resulted in northern Sinagua people moving to the Verde Valley. But the cliff dwelling, as it is seen today, was not constructed until the 1200s, when populations throughout the region were again shifting, this time because of drought.

Montezuma Castle.

The "castle," sheltered under a deep overhang in the cliff's face, is built of small limestone blocks laid in mud mortar and roofed by sycamore timbers overlaid by poles, sticks, grass, and several inches of mud. Observers today can only imagine the effort required to haul these heavy materials up the cliff. The outside rooms sit nearly flush with the high ledges and form a concave arc that conforms to the surrounding cave. A hundred feet below flows Beaver Creek, the life force of this community.

Two paths, one from the valley floor, which required the use of ladders, and one from along the side of the cliff, joined to enter the cliff dwelling. At the junction sits a small smoke-blackened room believed to have been a sentry post. Compact inner rooms with small doorways conserved heat and made hostile entry all but impossible. Two other factors enhanced heating: the site faces south and sits far above the colder air that settles on the valley floor below. While excavated remains of corn, beans, squash, and cotton point to agriculture, other plant remains, such as seeds, nuts, and agave, indicate that the Sinagua who lived here continued to forage.

The castle had a relatively brief occupancy. Scholars do not yet understand why the Sinagua left the seemingly ideal conditions of the Verde Valley. In drought conditions, this would have been a natural gathering place. Perhaps internal dissension developed, or disease, worsened by unsanitary conditions around the pueblos, reduced population. Future research may shed light on why the Sinagua abandoned Montezuma Castle and the valley.

In the 1880s, when the science of archaeology was barely in its infancy, Montezuma Castle was stripped of its well-preserved contents by a collector from nearby Fort Verde. Castle A, which is located 100 yards away at the base of the cliff, however, was more scientifically excavated in 1933–1934. This once five-storied pueblo (twice the size of Montezuma Castle) collapsed in a conflagration near the end of its occupation. Excavators found many burials here, one of which held a stunning array of jewelry. The dead person, a woman in her thirties, must have been held in special regard by the community.

Because of its fragility, the castle may no longer be entered. A paved pathway about a quarter of a mile long leads from the visitor center to an excellent viewpoint, continues on to Castle A, and loops back along Beaver Creek. It is an easy, pleasant walk. You should plan to spend at least half an hour on the whole tour, longer if you are inclined to relax in the shade of the sycamore trees along the way. And do not expect to be alone; the monument accommodates hundreds of visitors each day.

Montezuma Well.

Montezuma Well

Montezuma Well, located six miles north of Montezuma Castle but part of the same monument, is certainly one of the most unusual geological spots in the Southwest. Four hundred and seventy feet in diameter, this limestone sink appears as a small spring-fed lake set in a deep round cavity atop a hill. Ducks swim on its serene surface and coots poke along its reedy shores. Through its outlet flow a million and a half gallons of water per day. It is little wonder that this was a popular spot for the Hoho-kam and Sinagua to live.

The area surrounding the well was first permanently settled by Hohokam in the A.D. 600s and remained inhabited—later by the Sinagua—though the 1400s. Naturally, the 1,000 gallons-per-minute flow from the well gave rise to a network of irrigation ditches to agricultural fields below. Population around the well probably peaked after A.D. 1300, when area residents drew together for security. This consolidation, combined with defensive building, suggests that they may have been reacting to some external threat.

At Montezuma Well, a short trail leads to the rim of the hill overlooking the lake and ruins. Here the trail divides: One branch winds down to the water's edge, passing by some small cliff ruins and the well's outlet; the other leads to a larger ruins complex on the rim. Visitors need at least an hour to explore both trails.

An interesting feature located along the road near Montezuma Well is the roofed-over remains of a Hohokam pithouse. Many pithouses have been excavated in the Southwest but few have been preserved. Although only the floor features remain to be seen, a cut-away scale model is on exhibit to illustrate how it originally appeared.

Travelers will find restaurants and accommodations near the monument, and campgrounds are maintained nearby. Tuzigoot National Monument (see p. 155), another major Sinagua ruin, is only twenty-seven miles to the east.

Suggested reading: *Ruins Along the River*, by Carle Hodge, Southwest Parks and Monuments Association, Tucson, Arizona, 1986.

Tonto National Monument

Tonto National Monument is located on Arizona 88, 2 miles east of Roosevelt and 28 miles northwest of Globe, Arizona. Driving time from Phoenix is about 2.5 hours.

From the Lower Ruin at Tonto National Monument, you can gaze down over the saguaro cacti on the hillside below and across the vastness of the Tonto Basin. Except for the distant expanse of Roosevelt Lake, the view is virtually the same as that enjoyed by the Salado occupants of these cliff dwellings 700 years ago; neither the climate nor vegetation has changed appreciably.

The Salado built their original homes close by their cultivated fields on the Salt River floodplain in the Tonto Basin. Hohokam people also lived in this valley and probably taught the Salado techniques of irrigation. The Salado raised crops of corn, pumpkins, squash, gourds, several varieties of beans, cotton, and grain amaranth. Acorns, agave, various types of cactus, catclaw, acacia beans, cocklebur seeds, hackberry, juniper berries, mesquite beans, yucca, wild grapes, and walnuts were some of the wild food plants that augmented the Salado diet.

In the mid-1200s, some of the Salado moved to impregnable cliff sites 1,000 feet in elevation and several miles distant above their crop lands. Here, in cliff recesses, they constructed the dwellings that are the centerpieces of Tonto National Monument. The Salado interacted with the Anasazi to the north, who probably stimulated their interest in cliff-house building. What motivated them to move so far from their fields is unknown. Perhaps they had to rely on upland food resources during this period.

Dry cave sites, with their excellent preservation of perishable materials, have considerable archaeological value, and the ruins of Tonto, despite sixty years of souvenir hunting by settlers, are no exception. Tonto's caves held many items that have helped reconstruct a picture of Salado life. Ethnobotanist Vorsila Bohrer reported, "the plant material [at Tonto] . . . is perfectly preserved. Dried lima beans look like ones that might have come in a cellophane package on the grocery shelf."

The monument's three major sites—Upper Ruin, Lower Ruin, and Lower Ruin Annex—yielded not only the ethnobotanical remains mentioned above but also textiles of cotton, yucca, and hair; plaited yucca leaf sandals; basketry; matting; and cordage. Researchers recovered a thirty-inch bow of netleaf hackberry (a tough shock-resistant wood), arrows, clubs, and such household items as fire-making equipment, fiber pot rests, brushes, torches, stirring sticks, tattoo needles, gums and adhesives, and spinning and weaving implements. Ceremonial objects found included

prayer sticks, charms, paint daubers, reed cigarettes, dice, and a ceremonial bow.

Visitors may hike up to Lower Ruin along a half-mile trail from the visitor center. A trail guide offers much helpful information on the identity of plants along the walk. The round-trip takes about forty-five minutes. Upper Ruin may be visited, too, but only by advance reservation and accompanied by a park ranger. Several cultural exhibits relating to the Tonto cliff dwellings are on display at the visitor center, and a picnic area is located near the parking lot. Food and lodging can be found at Roosevelt, and there are numerous nearby camping spots.

An additional attraction of the Tonto area is the scenic drive on Arizona 88 from Apache Junction to Roosevelt. This tortuous, partly unpaved road offers some of the best desert-mountain views in the Southwest. Travelers should be warned, however, that some sections of the road are closed to vehicles over thirty feet in length, and you can only drive at an average of twenty to thirty miles per hour.

> Suggested reading: *Archaeological Studies at Tonto National Monument, Arizona*, by Charlie R. Steen, et al., Southwestern Monuments Association, Gila Pueblo, Globe, Arizona, 1962.

Besh Ba Gowah Archaeological Park

Besh Ba Gowah Archaeological Park is located along Jess Hayes Road, approximately 1.5 miles southwest of Globe, Arizona. Globe is 87 miles east of Phoenix along U.S. 60. To reach the site, follow South Broad Street to Ice House Canyon Road and continue to the Besh Ba Gowah turnoff on the right.

Besh Ba Gowah is an Apache phrase meaning "metal camp" or "place of metal" and refers to the intensive copper mining operations in the Globe area in historic times. Besh Ba Gowah ruins, however, is a Salado village site consisting of around 250 ground floor rooms and several plazas. The village may have contained as many as 450 total rooms when it was occupied between A.D. 1225 and 1450. Thus, it represents a major regional archaeological resource.

The village sits on a ridge overlooking Pinal Creek, a tributary of the Salt River, and is surrounded by the 8,000-foot Pinal Mountains to the southwest and the Apache Mountains to the north. The presence of numerous other ruins in the vicinity testifies to a

---

Lower Ruins, Tonto National Monument.

Besh Ba Gowah Ruins.

large prehistoric Indian population.

Besh Ba Gowah's buildings were constructed of unshaped granite cobbles set in thick clay mortar. Excavations have uncovered many small rooms believed to have been used for storage, many larger residential rooms (averaging 15 by 15 feet), and some even larger rooms of unknown function. The presence at the site of stored beans and corn, as well as many stone hoes, indicates that its inhabitants farmed, probably in fields along Pinal Creek. They were also fine craftspeople and traded actively with other villages in the area, as well as with people who lived as far away as Mexico and the Pacific Coast.

Salado culture is considered a blend of native or local traditions with influences from the Hohokam and Pueblo cultures. The presence at Besh Ba Gowah of a Hohokam component underneath the visible Salado village testifies to an earlier Hohokam presence. Archaeologists have yet to agree on the exact relationship between these two groups.

Besh Ba Gowah was originally surveyed and recorded by Adolph F. Bandelier in 1883, while he was waiting in Globe for threats of Apache attacks to subside before continuing his explorations. Bandelier identified the site's Salado character through its ceramics. Irene S. Vickrey conducted the first formal archaeological investigations at the site beginning in 1935 as a Federal Emergency Relief Administration project. Vickrey excavated over 100 rooms and recovered 350 Salado burials; however, she died before publishing the results of her work, and for many years, the ruins lay unattended and little appreciated.

In 1948, the Boy Scouts of America selected Besh Ba Gowah ruins as the site for their national jamboree, and in order to accommodate their camping needs, the Army Corps of Engineers bulldozed and leveled the northern portion of the site. The City of Globe subsequently developed this area into a city park and later bulldozed more of the ruins to make room for recreational facilities.

In 1984, with the area's mining economy in decline, the city began redeveloping the site and park complex to attract tourists. To carry out this plan, it engaged the services of professional archaeologists. Under the direction of John W. Hohmann, the site was mapped, excavated, stabilized, and partially reconstructed. In addition, a museum was built, and an interpretive trail through the ruins was created. The museum contains a reconstructed model of the pueblo, numerous examples of Gila Polychrome and other types of regionally made pottery, and prehistoric implements. One notable feature along the path is a large square subterranean room with benches along the wall that was used for religious ceremonies. It had an altar and a *sipapu* (symbolic entrance hole to the underworld), which was found filled with ground turquoise and sealed with a large quartz crystal.

The recent transformation of Besh Ba Gowah ruins from overgrown and vandalized mounds to an interpreted archaeological park reflects the growing public interest and pride in America's rich cultural heritage. Today, Besh Ba Gowah is a rewarding place to visit where you can learn much about the little-known Salado culture.

Travel services are available in Globe, and visitors may be interested in making a short side trip to another Salado ruins at Tonto National Monument (see p. 163).

Suggested reading: "Besh Ba Gowah," by Irene Vickrey, *The Kiva*, vol. 4, no. 5, 1939.

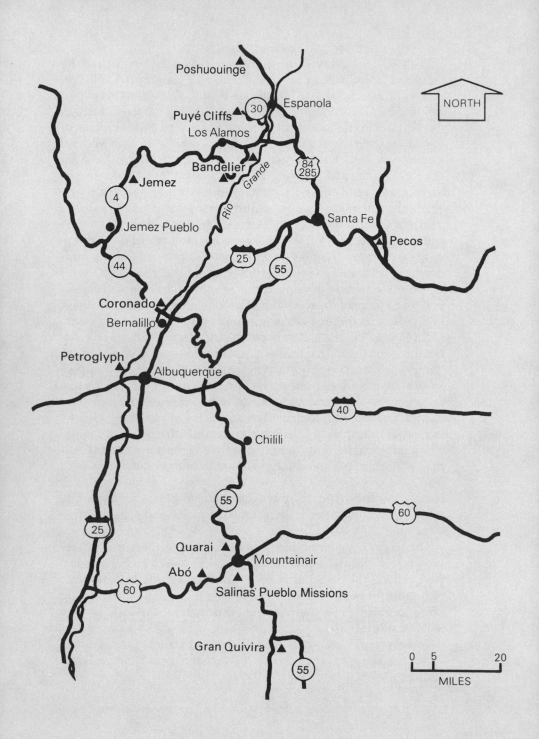

Poshuouinge ▲

🔵30 Espanola

Puyé Cliffs ▲
Los Alamos

Bandelier ▲

▲ Jemez
🔵4

● Jemez Pueblo

🛡84 285

Santa Fe ●

▲ Pecos

🔵44

🛡25 🔵55

Coronado ▲
Bernalillo ●

Petroglyph ▲

Albuquerque ●

🛡40

● Chilili

🔵55

🛡25

🛡60

🛡60

Quarai ▲

Abó ▲

Mountainair ●

▲ Salinas Pueblo Missions

Gran Quivira ▲

🔵55

NORTH

0   5   20
MILES

Rio Grande Area

PUEBLOS AND MISSIONS OF NEW MEXICO

I t is hard to visualize what life was like for the Spaniards who explored the American Southwest 400 years ago. It is even more difficult to imagine the impact that these mounted, armored soldiers made on the indigenous peoples they encountered along their marches. But to be at Pecos or Quarai today and lay your hand on the adobe and stone ruins of missions and pueblos is to feel the past literally at your fingertips. While intervening centuries may not melt away, the past attains an immediacy and substance that no historical writing can simulate.

The first contact between Pueblo Indian and European came in 1539, two and a half centuries after the Anasazi had abandoned their San Juan homeland, when Estebanico, Fray Marcos de Niza's guide, entered the Zuni pueblo of Hawikuh. Fray Marcos and his small party were on a reconnaissance mission to confirm rumors of riches in the northern territory.

Estebanico did not survive more than a few hours at Hawikuh, and his misfortune set Fray Marcos on a hasty return to Mexico City, where he became a celebrity by reporting, no doubt with exaggeration, his discovery of the Seven Cities of Cibola. The following year, with Fray Marcos guiding, Francisco Vasquez de Coronado led an army of soldiers, priests, and Indian allies back to Cibola to be the first to lay hands on its fabled wealth. When they arrived at Hawikuh, they observed, with unmitigated disappointment, not a city of gold but a pueblo built of mud and stone. Coronado's army attacked and overwhelmed the village but stayed only long enough to rest and recover before pursuing its fruitless quest to the Rio Grande Valley and beyond.

Although a few parties of explorers did penetrate Pueblo country

Pueblo petroglyph of Spanish horseman.

in the 1580s and 1590s, the Indians had no further European contact until 1598 when the king of Spain approved a contract with Juan de Oñate to establish a permanent colony in New Mexico at his own expense. While Oñate's official directive was to pacify and Christianize the Indians, he had an additional goal of personal enrichment. Like Coronado before him, Oñate soon developed an adversarial relationship with the Pueblos, coercing them to submit to his authority and to contribute food and supplies to sustain his impoverished followers. In his decade as New Mexico's first governor, he obtained pledges of allegiance and obedience from Pueblo *caciques* (religious leaders) and laid claim to some 87,000 square miles of territory in the name of the king. At the same time, his religious counterparts claimed thousands of souls for Christ. What these pledges, conversions, and claims actually meant to the natives was not recorded and was probably unknown to Spanish chroniclers.

The early explorers recorded seventy or more Pueblo villages whose inhabitants, while speaking half a dozen mutually unintelligible languages, shared many common traditions and beliefs. They lived in small autonomous *pueblos* or villages that were not politically or militarily allied with one other. Consequently, relatively small armed and mounted Spanish forces were able to dominate a large population of Indians by a strategy of pueblo-by-pueblo conquest.

The typical Rio Grande pueblo of the period was a compact community with large adobe or stone apartment houses built around a central court. There were few, if any, exterior doorways, and residents usually gained entrance through a single gateway.

To enter their homes, they would mount ladders from the plaza to the roofs and then descend through hatchways. Interior groups of rooms were interconnected by small doorways. Storage rooms tended to be on the first floor, living rooms in the upper stories, and work and play areas on the rooftops or in the plazas. The overall design was compact and efficient and accommodated potential defensive needs.

Like their Anasazi ancestors, the Pueblos were accomplished farmers, growing such staples as corn, various types of beans, squash, and pumpkins. They frequently raised turkeys in pens bordering the plazas, and they continued a long tradition of hunting and gathering. Their clothing was fashioned from deerskins and woven textiles, and in winter, they slept under feather blankets. Like all native peoples who live close to the land, they had a detailed knowledge and understanding of the natural environment and how they could use it to their benefit. Underlying this relationship was a strong religion based on living in harmony with nature and bringing rains to water their crops.

Rio Grande Pueblo culture, which originally developed from a Mogollon base, received a substantial impetus in the thirteeth and fourteenth centuries with the immigration of many dislocated Anasazi from the north and west. By the 1500s, the Pueblos had achieved a substantial population and a level of agricultural prosperity that became the target of the needy newcomers from Europe.

The Pueblos were not the only Native Americans in the Southwest. In 1540, Coronado had heard stories of attacks by nomadic Indians that had occurred twenty years earlier at some eastern villages. In fact, nomadic hunters from the Great Plains had shortly preceded the Spanish *entrada*. One of these groups was the *Apaches de Nabajo*, later to become the Navajo Nation.

The Pueblos, successful farmers that they were, soon found themselves pressured between two demanding and often hostile forces. Complex relationships between these competing groups began to develop and change as circumstances required. After harvests were gathered, the Plains tribes sometimes raided pueblos and attacked Spanish settlements, but at other times they carried on an active trade with the Pueblos. The Spaniards established an institution known as the *encomienda*. Under this system, a Spanish soldier-settler was granted the right to collect tribute from a group of Indians, usually in the form of set amounts of textiles, corn, buckskins, piñon nuts, or labor. In return, he promised protection from marauding enemies.

As the Spanish colony grew in size, Franciscan priests ventured farther into the hinterlands to establish missions, built with Indian labor, at such places as Abó (see p. 201), Quarai (see p. 199), Gran Quivira (see p. 196), Pecos (see p. 192), and Jemez (see p. 203).

The Franciscans were dedicated, courageous, enterprising men who carried out their missions with remarkable perseverance. Today, the ruins of their churches bear somber testimony to the organizational and architectural capabilities of these colonial missionaries.

The Pueblos fared less well. To better control them, the Spanish authorities consolidated their scattered communities into concentrated villages close to the missions. These pueblos were more vulnerable to epidemics of European diseases. Their reserves of food gradually disappeared under the tribute system, and much of their labor was spent fulfilling Spanish rather than Indian needs. Potentially useful European introductions such as guns, metal, and horses were denied them, and many of their religious ceremonies were suppressed. By the mid-1600s, the Pueblos had become impoverished, demoralized, and devastated by pestilence, Spanish demands, and Apache depredations. When drought struck in the late 1660s, their plight grew truly desperate.

During the same period, a power struggle arose between Spanish civil and ecclesiastical authorities, who disputed over such matters as the distribution of goods and services extracted from the Indians. Despite the *encomienda*, the Spanish colony, too, suffered from the adverse climatic conditions that were contributing to the faltering economy. Hardships and tensions throughout the territory mounted, and the people awaited some inevitable resolution.

The reckoning arrived with a fury on 10 August 1680, when the Pueblo Indians from Zuni to Taos arose in revolt against the Spanish colonists and priests. The uprising was brilliantly planned and coordinated. In concert, the Indians attacked settlements and drove out their occupants, killed priests and set fire to their churches, and laid seige to Santa Fe. Led by a San Juan mystic named Popé, this first and only pan-Pueblo uprising succeeded in liberating the region from its European overlords. It has been called "The First American Revolution." In the process, some 400 Spaniards lost their lives. The remainder of the colony retreated to El Paso where they were joined by some Indians from southern villages who had not participated in the rebellion. Here they regrouped and remained for twelve years before coming back to reconquer the territory under the leadership of Don Diego de Vargas.

The revolt and reconquest were deeply traumatic experiences for both the Spanish and the Indians. For the Indians, unification was ephemeral, and Pueblo life up and down the Rio Grande was profoundly changed. Some pueblos, such as San Marcos and Cienega, were abandoned, and others, such as Laguna, were founded. Many groups became refugees, moving far away to

Doorway at Pecos Ruins.

Pueblo kiva mural, Coronado State Monument.

live with the Hopis or Navajos. On their return, the Spanish substantially reformed their relationship with the Pueblos. They discontinued the *encomienda* and showed more tolerance for native religious practices and beliefs. Although missionary efforts resumed, the Spaniards interfered less in Indian life and made cooperative arrangements, particularly to defend against marauding Comanches.

Each Indian pueblo received from the Spanish king a land grant immediately surrounding the pueblo; these grants, however, did not take into account the more extensive territories long used by the Indians for economic and religious purposes. Through the eighteenth and early nineteenth centuries, as Spanish and Mexican settlements spread farther afield, lands traditionally belonging to the Pueblos and Navajos gradually diminished.

In 1846, New Mexico became a territory of the United States, and while life in Santa Fe and other towns changed dramatically, few meaningful developments reached the rural Indian and Hispanic communities. More pervasive change did arrive, however, with the coming of the railroad four decades later.

It was not until after the turn of the twentieth century that a few influential Anglo-Americans turned their attention to the Indian and Spanish ruins that had weathered the tumultuous events of past centuries. The most adamant preservationist was a Santa Fe–based archaeologist and entrepreneur named Edgar Lee Hewett. Hewett not only lobbied successfully for the passage of federal legislation to protect archaeological areas but also created programs to study these areas and trained many of the foremost figures in southwestern archaeology.

> Suggested reading: *Pueblos, Villages, Forts, and Trails: A Guide to New Mexico's Past*, by David Grant Noble, University of New Mexico Press, Albuquerque, New Mexico, 1994.

Bandelier National Monument

Bandelier National Monument is located near Los Alamos, New Mexico, 46 miles west of Santa Fe. From Santa Fe, take U.S. 285 north to Pojoaque, then bear left on New Mexico 4 and continue 24 miles to the monument.

Bandelier National Monument owes its name to Adolph F. Bandelier (1840–1914), a legendary figure among southwestern archaeologists, ethnographers, and historians. In 1880, this Swiss-born Illinois businessman with a consuming passion for studying Native American cultures, arrived in Santa Fe to begin a truly phenomenal career as a researcher and explorer. Under the auspices of the Archaeological Institute of America, his mission was to study the Indian tribes of the Southwest, a land whose natives were little understood by the dominant Anglo-American society. Surviving on a small allowance, Bandelier covered great distances on foot, often overcoming formidable obstacles, such as weather, terrain, fatigue, and sickness. His pioneering efforts as an observer of customs, recorder of story and myth, and surveyor of prehistoric ruins established him as the first anthropological scholar of the American Southwest.

With a guide from Cochiti Pueblo, Bandelier arrived at what is now his namesake monument on 23 October 1880. He was highly impressed by his first view of the place and scribbled in his journal, "The grandest thing I ever saw. A magnificent growth of pines, encina [oak], alamos [poplars], and towering cliffs, of pumice or volcanic tuff, exceedingly friable." He went on to describe the impressive ruins he encountered. "There are some of one, two, and three stories. In most cases the plaster is still in the rooms. Some are walled in; others are mere holes in the rocks." Bandelier's *Southwestern Journals*, only one of his many contributions to anthropological literature, were published in 1966–1976. Bandelier eventually left New Mexico to work in Peru. In 1914, he died in Seville, Spain, while conducting documentary research, and since his wife was penniless at the time of his death, he was buried there. Many years later, a group of Bandelier loyalists in Santa Fe arranged to have his bones returned to New Mexico, and

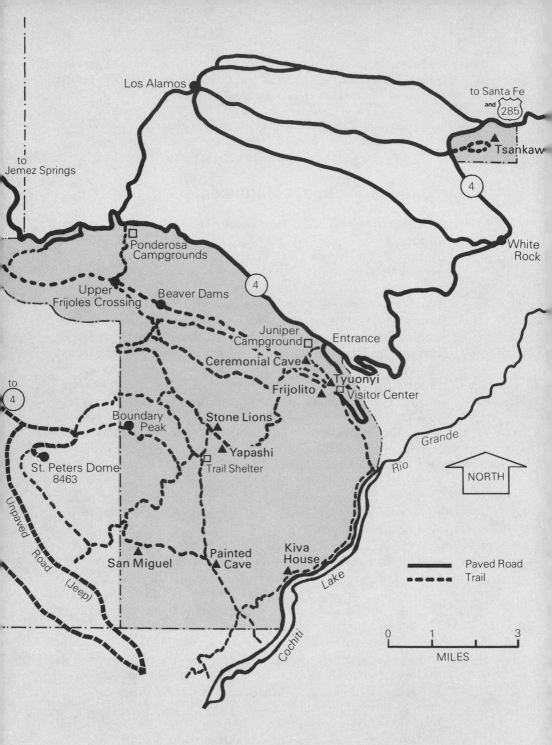

Los Alamos

to Jemez Springs

285

4

Tsankaw

White Rock

Ponderosa Campgrounds

Upper Frijoles Crossing

Beaver Dams

4

Juniper Campground

Entrance

Ceremonial Cave

Tyuonyi

Frijolito

Visitor Center

to 4

Boundary Peak

Stone Lions

Yapashi

St. Peters Dome 8463

Trail Shelter

Grande

Rio

NORTH

San Miguel

Painted Cave

Kiva House

Unpaved Road (Jeep)

Lake

Cochiti

Paved Road

Trail

0   1   3

MILES

Bandelier National Monument

Tyuonyi Ruins, Bandelier National Monument.

on 16 October 1980, his ashes were scattered at a spot overlooking Frijoles Canyon, which had so impressed him 100 years before.

The prehistory of the Pajarito Plateau, on which Bandelier National Monument is situated, begins thousands of years before the Christian era, when nomadic big-game hunters roamed across most of the North American continent. The discovery of several of their distinctive spear points indicates their occasional presence in the area. But the first documented evidence that Indians were living near the monument is in the form of Archaic campsites, such as Ojala Cave and others among sand dunes along the Rio Grande. The earliest precisely dated site was occupied about 2010 B.C., with later sites dating between 670 and 590 B.C. The Archaic people moved about in family groups, hunting game and harvesting seeds, nuts, and fruits that ripened in different areas at different times of the year.

Pueblo Indians first lived permanently on the Pajarito Plateau in the late twelfth century after the collapse of the Chaco system to the west and the subsequent movement of peoples into the Rio Grande Valley. They lived in single-family dwellings or small hamlets housing no more than two or three families, and they moved their households every few years as they sought out new fields to farm.

By A.D. 1300, as the Anasazi abandoned the Four Corners region, the Rio Grande population dramatically increased and

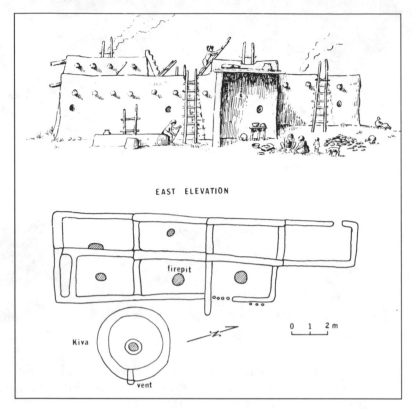

EAST ELEVATION

firepit

Kiva

vent

0   1   2 m

Typical pueblo site on the Pajarito Plateau, ca. A.D. 1175–1300.
Drawing by Richard W. Lang. Courtesy School of American Research.

the numbers of Indians living on the Pajarito swelled. Tyuonyi,
the circular pueblo ruins on the floor of Frijoles Canyon, is a
good example of one of the larger sites built during this period.
Other pueblos, such as Tserige, Otowi, and Puyé, which are outside the monument boundaries, were even larger and indicate a
significant consolidation of the population. Frequently, these
large pueblos were planned around a central plaza with apartments stepped back to a height of several stories.

The Indians also built many small pueblos on the mesas, which
archaeologists believe probably served as convenient summer
residences for those responsible for raising crops. The Pajaritans
expanded natural concavities along the soft tuff cliffs into cozy
rooms and kivas. In front of these, they built multistoried pueblos
to accommodate the growing population. The most popular trail
at Bandelier runs through Tyuonyi and winds up the talus slope
past dozens of carved-out chambers, some of which visitors can
enter by ladders.

Many of the Pajarito pueblos are connected by a network of

Cave dwelling in Frijoles Canyon.

prehistoric trails, some of which are sunken more than a foot into the rock. The depth of such trail segments suggests that more than foot-traffic abrasion was at work. Some researchers have speculated that they had a ceremonial function. One of these trails leads to Tsankawi Pueblo in a separate unit of the monument and is still used today by visitors to this site.

Life in Frijoles Canyon centered around raising corn, beans, and squash along the bottom lands, perhaps using small-scale irrigation. Water, both as rain and runoff was plentiful, and mesa-top gardens often were watered by the use of small check dams. The Jemez Mountains were rich in game, and the varied natural environment offered a wealth of plant foods. Under these favorable conditions, Pajaritan culture flourished for nearly three centuries.

No one really understands why the Pueblo Indians left Frijoles Canyon and the Pajarito Plateau in the early 1500s. Spaniards first arrived in this part of the Rio Grande Valley in 1541, and they established a colony at San Juan Pueblo half a century later. It is possible that contagious European diseases were carried into the region by Indian traders a generation before the actual arrival of the conquistadores. Such a disaster may in some way have brought about an abandonment of the Pajarito pueblos. Future archaeological research may shed light on this interesting question.

The descendents of the Pajarito people presently live along the Rio Grande, and there is reason to believe that the Anasazi, who once inhabited the portions of the Pajarito Plateau north of Frijoles Canyon, were the ancestors of the modern-day Tewa-speaking Indians of Santa Clara and San Ildefonso pueblos. The residents of Cochiti and Santo Domingo are likely descended from the southern Pajaritans.

Bandelier National Monument offers a variety of activities for visitors. In a couple of hours, you can see the exhibits at the visitor center, visit Tyuonyi, and take the interpretive trail to the cave dwellings. The round-trip to Ceremonial Cave, which itself is reached by means of a series of ladders up the cliff, takes another hour or so. Visitors can also hike down canyon to the Rio Grande or follow the mile-long trail to the Frijolito Ruin. Other more distant archaeological sites include the Stone Lions shrine (twelve miles round-trip), Painted Cave (twenty miles round-trip), and the pueblos of San Miguel, Yapashi, and Kiva House, all requiring long hikes. Also of interest is Tsankawi, located in a separate unit of the monument, along Route 4, eleven miles north of the main monument entrance. Look for the Tsankawi turnoff on the left-hand side of the road when driving to the monument from Santa Fe. Tsankawi sits on a prominent mesa with a spectacular view over the entire region. The trail passes over the unexcavated ruins of Tsankawi Pueblo and loops around

Prehistoric Indian trail to Tsankawi Ruins. Trail was cut or worn into the soft volcanic rock.

a series of cave dwellings similar to those of Frijoles Canyon.

The Pajarito Plateau is a fascinating natural environment of considerable beauty and an area of much cultural interest. At the monument, you can also learn about the region's turbulent geologic history, which includes episodes of volcanic eruptions and faulting, as well as the dramatic erosion that formed Frijoles and other canyons.

Facilities at the monument include a campground on the mesa, a picnic area along Frijoles Creek, and a snack bar and gift shop. Overnight lodgings are available in Los Alamos and Española. Another major ruin in the vicinity is Puyé Cliff Dwellings (see following pages) on the Santa Clara Indian Reservation.

Suggested reading: *The Delight Makers,* by Adolph F. Bandelier, Harcourt Brace Jovanovich, New York, 1971. *Bandelier National Monument,* by Patricia Barry, Southwest Parks and Monuments Association, Tucson, Arizona, 1990.

Puyé Cliff Dwellings

Puyé Cliff Dwellings are located on the Santa Clara Indian Reservation south of Española, New Mexico. From Española, take New Mexico 30 south for 5 miles, then turn west and proceed another 7 miles to the ruins, which are managed by the Santa Clara tribe.

Puyé (poo-yay) is one of several very large late-prehistoric pueblos on the Pajarito Plateau. Culturally, its story parallels that of the pueblos and cliff dwellings of nearby Bandelier National Monument (see p. 175). Like Bandelier, Puyé is situated on the eastern flank of the Jemez volcanic field. A little over one million years ago, two catastrophic eruptions occurred in the Jemez Mountains in which hundreds of cubic miles of volcanic ash were spewed over a large area to form a flat sloping plateau with deep deposits of tuff, a pumiceous rock. Over the next million years, streams flowing down from the mountains cut the canyons that embrace Puyé Mesa and other canyons across the entire plateau. This well-watered canyon and mesa country, spanning a varied environment, from the cool forested highlands to the warmer Rio Grande Valley, became an ideally suited place for human beings to inhabit.

The northern sector of the Pajarito Plateau, where Puyé is located, saw its first permanent Puebloan settlements in the 1200s, when population throughout the northern Rio Grande Valley was increasing. In the 1300s, the Pajaritan farmers began to consolidate into larger pueblos, sometimes two-storied and shaped like a horseshoe with the opening facing east. Still later, the village builders closed the horseshoe, creating a plaza with a kiva surrounded on all sides by terraced apartments. In the 1400s, the trend to larger communities reached a peak when the northern Pajaritan population congregated in five towns: Tsankawi, Tserige, Navawi, Otowi, and Puyé. Puyé, one of the largest, had more than 1,000 rooms.

Puyé Pueblo, which sits on top of the mesa, was built of blocks of tuff that the Indians shaped with stone tools. Its multistoried quadrangle of apartments was stepped back to form a protected inner court in which the people worked, played, raised turkeys, and performed religious ceremonies. The limited access to the plaza also offered a degree of defense against potential enemies. Below the edge of the mesa, the Puyé residents built more apartments with back rooms excavated into the friable rock. These cliff dwellings, which extend for at least a mile, housed many more people. Over the centuries since Puyé was abandoned, the cliffside buildings have fallen down, but the cave rooms remain and may be explored by visitors. One group of rooms along the

Puyé Ruins.

cliff has been reconstructed.

Like the residents of Frijoles Canyon at Bandelier, the Puyé Indians grew corn, beans, and squash below their dwellings, making use of the creek that flows out of Santa Clara Canyon to irrigate their garden plots. They hunted deer in the Jemez Mountains and rabbits in the piñon-juniper woodlands and probably caught fish in the Rio Grande.

Puyé Pueblo was partially excavated in 1907 by Edgar Lee Hewett under the auspices of the Southwest Society of the

Archaeological Institute of America. Two years later, Sylvanus G. Morley excavated South House at Puyé. These were the first systematic archaeological excavations to take place in the Rio Grande region, but unfortunately, only general descriptive notes were kept, and no detailed report was ever published. In these early years of archaeological science, emphasis was placed more on opening ruins and collecting artifacts than on trying to reconstruct the dynamics of human behavior.

Puyé and other towns on the Pajarito were abandoned in the 1500s, shortly before the arrival of Spaniards in New Mexico. The inhabitants of Puyé reestablished themselves closer to the Rio Grande, probably at the site of Santa Clara Pueblo. The Santa Clarans manage the site and regard Puyé as an ancestral pueblo.

Visitors can walk to the cliff dwellings from Puyé's lower parking lot and climb by footpath to the top of the mesa. You can also drive up a winding road to a parking area on the mesa adjacent to Puyé Pueblo. The lower walls of the pueblo have been rebuilt to give visitors a visual, though somewhat unauthentic, impression of the full extent of the village. One kiva also has been restored and may be entered through a rooftop hatchway. Little archaeological or cultural interpretation is offered at the site.

The park at Puyé Cliff Dwellings has drinking water, toilets, and a picnic area, and camping is available at nearby Santa Clara Canyon. Travel services are available in Española, Los Alamos, and Santa Fe.

> Suggested reading: *Pajarito Plateau Archaeological Survey and Excavations,* by Charlie R. Steen, The Los Alamos Scientific Laboratory of the University of California, Los Alamos, New Mexico, 1977.

Poshuouinge

Poshuouinge is located along U.S. 84, 2.5 miles south of Abiquiu, New Mexico. A short trail leads to the ruins from a well-marked highway turnoff.

Poshuouinge (poshu-wingay), a large site in the lower Chama River Valley, is ancestral to the Tewa Indians who now live at the pueblos of San Ildefonso, San Juan, Santa Clara, and Nambé. Although some researchers hold the view that the Chama served as a corridor of migration from the Four Corners region, the archaeological evidence suggests that sites like Poshuouinge were settled by an overflow population in the Rio Grande Valley itself. The pueblo was founded about A.D. 1400 and by 1450 it had become a thriving village, one of many scattered along the river.

The Chama Valley offered some distinct advantages to the Anasazi. Water was plentiful, and the floodplains were suitable for farming. In addition, the nearby uplands and mountains offered good foraging and hunting. No doubt the population grew as a result of productive agriculture, as well as from immigration. As their communities swelled, the people developed a new and innovative farming technique. While still cultivating the floodplains, they also began dry-farming crops adjacent to their villages. Gardens were carefully laid out in grids, and river cobbles were used as a mulch to help preserve moisture and increase soil temperatures. Archaeologists have found literally hundreds of acres covered by these cobbled gardens.

Poshuouinge survived until A.D. 1500 or so when many of the Chama Valley inhabitants began moving to the valley of the Rio Grande. Some Chama Valley towns probably were still thriving when Coronado explored the Rio Grande Valley in 1540–1541.

Adolph F. Bandelier, the famous explorer/anthropologist visited Poshuouinge in 1885, and J. A. Jeancon excavated 137 rooms in 1919. Jeancon's excavation report contains an interesting inventory of artifacts he unearthed. He lists many stone tools, such as polishing stones for floors, "andirons," mortars, and arrow shaft polishers. Bone implements included awls, tanning tools, breastplates, turkey calls and flutes, spatulas, and knives. He uncovered ceramic pipes, dishes and vessels, gaming pieces, spindle whorls, and pot lids. Fetishes, ceramic cloud blowers, and lightning stones were among the ceremonial items found. Lightning stones are usually small, smooth whitish stones, which, when rubbed together in the dark, produce a faint flickering light that resembles distant lightning.

Poshuouinge has 700 ground-floor rooms that surround two large plazas. A large kiva is clearly visible within the larger plaza. The adobe pueblo was mostly two-storied, although some parts had but a single story, and others probably were three-tiered. Grid gardens were cultivated just to the east of the village.

A short trail from the parking area leads up the mesa past the pueblo ruins to a good viewpoint above. The U. S. Forest Service, which maintains the site, has placed several interpretive signs along the path. The complete walk takes about half an hour.

Food and gas are available along the highway, in Abiquiu, and to the south in Española. Abiquiu itself is a historic Spanish-American village just off the highway and was the home of the renowned painter, Georgia O'Keeffe.

Suggested reading: *Excavations in the Chama Valley, New Mexico*, by J. A. Jeancon, Bureau of American Ethnology Bulletin 81, Smithsonian Institution, Washington, D.C., 1923.

Petroglyph National Monument

Petroglyph National Monument is presently being developed along the West Mesa of Albuquerque, New Mexico. Areas that are now open include the Piedras Marcadas Area, Indian Petroglyph State Park, Rinconada Canyon, and the Geologic Windows. Until a visitor center is established and road signs are in place, visitors wishing to see this extensive collection of rock art should contact the monument's offices at 123 4th Street S.W., Room 101, in Albuquerque, (505) 766-8375. To contact the ranger station, please call (505) 839-4429.

The city of Albuquerque has long maintained a small petroglyph park on Atrisco Drive (Unser Boulevard on some maps) northwest of downtown Albuquerque, and this park constitutes one section of the national monument. To reach this area, drive north on Coors Boulevard to Montano Road; turn left on Montano and proceed 2 miles to Atrisco (Unser); turn right on Atrisco and continue 0.5 miles to the park's entrance.

Petroglyph National Monument was established in 1990 to protect and interpret one of the Southwest's largest collections of Indian rock art. People with an interest in geology and volcanoes also will find much to explore here. The petroglyphs, numbering over 15,000 within the 7,000-acre monument, are scattered in numerous areas along the seventeen-mile escarpment of Albuquerque's West Mesa. As the monument develops an interpretive program, visitors will be able to hike along trails past many concentrations of petroglyphs.

While some petroglyphs in the national monument probably date to the late Archaic period, at least 3,000 years ago, most were made by Pueblo Indians who lived in the Rio Grande Valley between about A.D. 1300 and 1680. The inhabitants of the pueblos in the Albuquerque area were Tiwa-speaking as are the present-day people of nearby Sandia and Isleta. It was among these communities that Coronado's army spent the winter of 1540–1541, and he called the region Tiguex Province. Even though the glyphs themselves are centuries old, modern-day Pueblo Indians still visit sacred sites and shrines among them.

The West Mesa petroglyphs were pecked or incised on basaltic boulders and low cliffs along the eastern edge of an extensive ancient lava flow that came from a series of volcanoes on the western edge of the monument. The oldest figures, dating from about 1000 B.C. to A.D. 500 are curvilinear abstract patterns, such as spirals and meandering lines. The great majority of the petroglyphs, however, date from A.D. 1350 to 1680 and include representations of human figures and faces (probably kachina masks)

Rock art at Petroglyph National Monument.

and humpbacked flute players; ceremonial figures, such as star beings and serpent beings; and a variety of creatures, such as dragon flies, lizards, snakes, large animals, and birds. In addition, Spanish-American sheepherders incised Christian crosses and their names on some rocks.

It is quite fascinating how these petroglyphs communicate the feelings and beliefs of preliterate people who lived long in the past. These images etched or pecked into the hard basalt are very enduring and many of them stand out boldly, as if they were recently executed.

What these ancient petroglyphs actually mean and why they were made is not well understood. The tradition of making rock art subsided after the Pueblo Revolt of 1680 and little of what contemporary Native Americans may know about the significance of the glyphs has been conveyed to people outside their own communities. Clearly, much rock art was inspired by religious beliefs. Kachina masks, for example, are worn at ceremonies to bring the spirit and power of the kachina deity to the pueblo. Some rock art scholars theorize that the horned serpent figures are local representations of the ancient Mexican god Quetzalcoatl. The connection between the Indians of the Rio Grande Valley and cultures far to the south also is evidenced in an image at Indian Petroglyph State Park (part of the national monument) depicting a caged parrot. Parrots, especially scarlet macaws, were traded north from Casas Grandes (see p. 8) and used for their plumage. Archaeologists have excavated burials of these exotic birds at numerous sites throughout the Southwest.

Petroglyph National Monument is administered cooperatively by the National Park Service, the state of New Mexico, and the city of Albuquerque. We are indeed fortunate that a group of interested citizens in Albuquerque lobbied for the creation of Petroglyph National Monument. In recent years, the West Mesa has been increasingly developed into subdivisions, and the petroglyph area was being degraded. As the monument develops, one of the world's largest concentrations of rock art will be available for the public to enjoy.

> Suggested reading: *Rock Art in New Mexico*, by Polly Schaafsma, New Mexico State Planning Office and the Museum of New Mexico Press, Santa Fe, New Mexico, 1972.

Coronado State Monument

Coronado State Monument is located along New Mexico 44, 1 mile west of Bernalillo, New Mexico.

The ruins of Kuaua Pueblo at Coronado State Monument lie on a windy rise of land overlooking the Rio Grande. Rolling prairies surround all sides, and the site has a clear view of the Sandia Mountains to the east. The low mud walls of the ruins, eroding under each passing storm, are a lingering reminder of the life and culture that flourished here for at least three centuries.

Kuaua is a fine archaeological example of a Rio Grande pueblo from the period before and after European-Pueblo contact. The pueblo dates to the fourteenth century, a time when many Anasazi groups from the west were migrating to the Rio Grande, and was abandoned in the early seventeenth century. The pueblo consisted of large multistoried adobe room blocks surrounding

Kuaua Ruins, Coronado State Monument.

three spacious plazas with underground kivas or ceremonial chambers. Like many Pueblo villages, Kuaua seems to have been designed with defense in mind. Its high exterior, doorless walls would have helped its inhabitants fend off any attack. In its prime, it was a formidable fortified town only accessible through narrow passageways that could have been barricaded.

The Kuauans probably were Tiwa-speaking Indians, ancestors of the present-day residents of Sandia and Isleta pueblos. They raised corn, beans, and squash in irrigated fields along the river and hunted in the nearby mountains where archaeologists have found examples of their characteristic glazeware pottery. The river was their life force, supplying water, attracting game, creating environments for a wide variety of edible plants, and linking the Kuauans to other pueblos up- and downstream.

The Spanish expedition led by Francisco Vasquez de Coronado spent the winter of 1540–1541 at the pueblo of Alcanfor, which was along the Rio Grande near present-day Bernalillo. Coronado's expeditionary force included 300 Spanish soldiers, 1,000 Indian allies and slaves, 1,000 horses, and 500 mules. In its historic exploration—the first by Europeans in the American Southwest—the expedition had traveled west from the land of the Zunis to intercept the Rio Grande near Isleta, just south of present-day Albuquerque. As the Spaniards worked their way north, they passed through this region, which they named the Province of Tiguex. Tiguex contained a dozen pueblos in a corridor along the river, one of which they named "Alcanfor." No evidence exists that Kuaua is the site; however, the two villages certainly were in close proximity to each other and members of Coronado's expedition must have visited Kuaua. When the Spaniards moved into Alcanfor, its Indian residents moved away, allowing the foreigners to use it for their winter quarters.

When Coronado arrived in Tiguex, his party had desperate needs. The pueblo sheltered his men, but they also demanded much food and clothing from their "hosts." As the days passed, the initially cordial relationship between the Spaniards and the inhabitants of Tiguex began to deteriorate. The situation was exacerbated when an Indian from the nearby village of Arenal accused a Spanish soldier of attacking his wife. The charge was dismissed by the Spaniards for lack of evidence. Eventually, open warfare broke out, and Coronado's forces conquered both Arenal and another pueblo called Moho. Many Indians lost their lives, and the adversarial relationship between Spaniard and Indian, which had begun at Zuni, became firmly embedded. It would culminate 140 years later in the Great Pueblo Revolt, after which Kuaua was abandoned.

Coronado's chronicler, Pedro de Castañeda, recorded his observations of pueblo building in 1540–1541: "They all work together to build the villages, the women being engaged in making the mixture and the walls, while the men bring the wood and put it in place. They have no lime, but they make a mixture of ashes, coals, and dirt which is almost as good as mortar, for when the house is to have four stories, they do not make the walls more than half a yard thick."

The Pueblos originally "puddled" the adobe mud on their walls in courses, allowing each course to set up before laying another on top. During the 1930s, archaeologists excavated 1,200 rooms at Kuaua. The partial restoration of much of the pueblo at this time accounts for the adobe bricks visitors see today in the wall construction.

The most significant find at Kuaua was the now-famous kiva with its seventeen layers of multicolored murals. This discovery represents the first extensive prehistoric mural art found in New Mexico. The kiva, which has been reconstructed with full-scale reproductions of the murals, may be entered by means of a ladder through the smokehole. Visitors who have been to Aztec Ruins (see p. 127) will be interested in comparing these two subter-

Reconstructed kiva at Kuaua.

ranean ceremonial structures, which represent differing expressions of Anasazi religious art and architecture.

Coronado State Monument's small museum includes cultural exhibits that are interesting to see prior to walking through the ruins. The adjacent state park has picnic tables and camping. Travelers could easily visit Kuaua Ruins and nearby Petroglyph National Monument (see p. 186) on the same day. Also of interest is the Maxwell Museum of Anthropology in Albuquerque with its fine permanent exhibit on the Southwest.

Suggested reading: *Narratives of the Coronado Expedition, 1540–1542,* by George P. Hammond and Agapito Rey, University of New Mexico Press, Albuquerque, New Mexico, 1940.

Pecos National Historical Park

Pecos National Historic Park is located off Interstate 25, approximately 25 miles east of Santa Fe, New Mexico. From Santa Fe, take the Glorieta-Pecos exit and proceed 8 miles through Pecos Village to the monument. Southbound travelers on the interstate should take the Rowe exit and continue 3 miles to the ruins.

In 1927, Alfred Vincent Kidder invited his colleagues to join him at Pecos Ruins to discuss common archaeological problems and concerns. Kidder was nearing the completion of his excavations at Pecos Ruins that had begun in 1915, a project that would become a landmark in the history of New World archaeology. In addition to holding wide-ranging discussions on the status of southwestern archaeology, Kidder's peers had an opportunity to witness the results of his detailed and systematic excavation methods. The Pecos Conference became an annual tradition among southwestern archaeolologists and continues to the present day.

Kidder's work at Pecos was described by the archaeologist and historian Richard B. Woodbury as "unprecedented in North American archaeology in its extended focus on a single site, its large scale, its careful planning and organization, and its use of specialists outside archaeology." The project marked a departure in archaeology from artifact collecting for museums to recovering and interpreting archaeological data in order to better understand cultural history.

Pecos Ruins are situated on a rocky knoll in the middle of a wide fertile valley. Nearby, the Pecos River flows out of the high mountains to the north and continues its long journey through New Mexico to join the Rio Grande in Texas. High mesas border the Pecos Valley on its south side, and to the west lies Glorieta Pass, a gateway to the Rio Grande Valley and the site of a significant Civil War battle. From the ruins, the valley descends gradually eastward, eventually opening out onto the southern Great Plains.

All of this geography, beyond providing the people of Pecos with a beautiful and varied environment, played a part in the life and history of the pueblo. Close by were fertile farmlands, reliable springs, and fuel wood; the high country was rich in game, plant resources, and timbers for building; and materials for making tools, weapons, pottery, and basketry were also close at hand. But what gave Pecos a special advantage was its strategic location between the agricultural Pueblo communities of the northern Rio Grande and the nomadic hunting tribes of the plains. Trade became a central factor in the pueblo's economy. In their role as middlemen, the Pecoseños acquired wealth, but not without cost, for they frequently found themselves the target of raids by

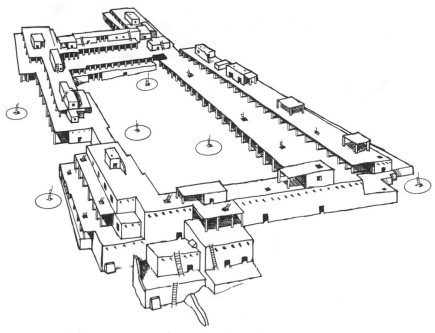

Reconstruction of North Pueblo, Pecos National Historic Park.

Apaches, Comanches, and Caddoans.

Pecos's history began after A.D. 800 when Puebloan settlers in the Rio Grande Valley moved into the upper Pecos Valley to form small, scattered pithouse hamlets. Over the centuries, the population slowly grew, but after A.D. 1200, it suddenly increased, probably as a result of immigration. The Forked Lightning Ruins, which is located in the monument, dates to this period, as does a pueblo underlying Pecos Ruins.

Pecos Pueblo was founded around A.D. 1300 and eventually grew to nearly 700 rooms arranged in a quadrangle of multilevel community houses around a central plaza. The pueblo was constructed like a fortress with high outside walls without doors. From its ramparts, Pecos warriors had a clear view in all directions. A perimeter wall provided an initial defensive line against attackers.

The inhabitants of Pecos were Towa-speaking Indians whose numbers eventually grew to 1,500 or 2,000 people. They were among the first North Americans to feel the impact of contact with Europeans. Less than fifty years after Columbus set foot in the New World, this pueblo was visited by the conquistador Francisco Vasquez de Coronado. Coronado came to Pecos after a trying and fruitless search for riches among the Zunis and Southern Tiwas. His bad reputation among Pueblo Indians to the west had no doubt preceded him, and the leaders of Pecos encouraged him to pursue his quest on the bleak windswept plains of eastern New Mexico and Nebraska.

After Coronado, Pecos was spared further contact with Spaniards until 1590, when Castaño de Sosa stormed and occupied the pueblo with a small, well-armed force. In his account of the expedition, de Sosa wrote that the pueblo was constructed of room blocks up to four stories in height, which the Indians reached by ladders that could be drawn up after them. De Sosa arrived in winter and noted that the men wore cotton blankets under a buffalo robe, and the women were dressed "with a blanket drawn in a knot at the shoulder and a sash the width of a palm at the waist." Over this they wore colorful blankets or turkey feather robes.

In 1618, Franciscan monks established a mission just east of Pecos Pueblo, which later included a massive adobe church and *convento* (living quarters of the padres) complete with carpenter shop, weaving rooms, tanneries, stable, school, and living quarters. The Franciscans introduced wheat, bread making, metal tools, new building methods, animal husbandry, and a religion that was revolutionary to the Indians. They also suppressed native religious practices. One of Kidder's findings was a cache of smashed clay figurines and a stone "idol" that had been broken and repaired.

The Pecos mission was destroyed in the Pueblo Revolt of 1680 but resurrected after the Spanish reconquest of 1693–1696 in which the Pecoseños allied themselves with Don Diego de Vargas. The eighteenth century was devastating to Pecos. Epidemics of fever, measles, smallpox, and other pestilences decimated the population, and the pueblo was repeatedly invaded by Apaches and Comanches. By the latter part of the century, Pecos's once proud 500-warrior army had been reduced to a shadow of its former strength, and the pueblo was dependent upon the Spanish for defense. A dwindling population, however, lingered at the pueblo into the nineteenth century. In 1838, seventeen weary souls, Pecos's last occupants, trekked eighty miles northwest to join relatives at Jemez Pueblo.

The most impressive ruins at Pecos are the standing remains of the eighteenth-century church, with its massive adobe walls and arched doorways. The footings of an older and even larger church are also visible. Visitors should stop first at the visitor center to see the monument's fine museum and pick up a trail guide. The trail leads up the hill to the ruins of the pueblo and mission. One kiva has been restored and may be entered by a ladder down the roof hatchway. The pueblo ruins, though in large part excavated in the 1920s, were backfilled to preserve the adobe walls, which are vulnerable to weathering. In summer, the monument has a "living history" program that includes demonstrations by native craftspeople.

Ruins of the Misión de Nuestra Senora de los Angeles de Porciuncula at Pecos National Historical Park.

Pecos National Historical Park is acquiring a portion of the adjacent Forked Lighting Ranch, whose additional Pueblo sites and historic ranch house will be incorporated into the park's interpretive program. In addition, the park administers the Civil War battlefield at Glorieta Pass. Further information on these new areas is available at the visitor center.

Pecos village, located about two miles from the ruins, has several restaurants, a grocery store, and gas station. From the village, visitors can drive north up the Pecos River canyon to camping and picnicking areas and good fishing spots. From Santa Fe, a trip to Pecos makes a very pleasant and interesting half-day excursion.

Suggested reading: *Kiva, Cross, and Crown: The Pecos Indians and New Mexico, 1540-1840,* by John L. Kessell, the National Park Service, Washington, D.C., 1979.

Salinas Pueblo Missions National Monument

Salinas Pueblo Missions National Monument consists of three separate pueblo and mission ruins—Gran Quivira, Quarai, and Abó—in central New Mexico. The monument's visitor center is located in Mountainair, at the corner of Broadway and Ripley streets.

The historic Spanish colonial province of Salinas lay in New Mexico's Estancia Valley and was named for a string of salt flats and shallow ephemeral lakes near present-day Willard. These "lakes" are the remnants of a large brackish body of water that flooded the valley in the last ice age. Eleven thousand years ago, Paleo-Indian hunters stalked mammoths and other now-extinct animals as they drank at watering holes in the valley. They were probably the first human beings to lay eyes on this part of the Southwest. Beyond their finely made Clovis spear points, which have been found embedded in the skeletons of the big game they hunted, they left little trace of their presence and almost nothing is known about them.

It was not until about A.D. 600 to 900, however, that the Salinas region saw permanent human occupants in any numbers. At that time, Indians moved here to live in simple pithouse hamlets. They made an unpainted reddish brown pottery in the Mogollon style. After a span of 200 years, they began building above-ground masonry pueblos, which were in the style of San Juan Anasazi structures built 300 years earlier. By A.D. 1300, the Salinas pueblos had grown to full-fledged apartment complexes. When the Spanish came in 1598, the largest Salinas town, Pueblo de las Humanas (later called Gran Quivira), rivaled Pecos in size and strength.

Gran Quivira

Gran Quivira is located 26 miles south of Mountainair on New Mexico 55.

Gran Quivira does not seem a likely spot for a town. No more exposed and windy spot within a ten-mile radius can be found, and water is scarce. The site, however, was inhabited by Tompiro-speaking Pueblo Indians who held a lively trade with buffalo hunters from the southern plains to the east. One of these hunting tribes was the Humanas after whom the pueblo was originally named by the Spanish. Evidently, the early Gran Quivira people also had ties with, and perhaps had origins among, the Mogollon Indians (see p. 1) to the southwest.

About 1545, the archaeological record reveals that a group of

The ruins at Gran Quivira.

immigrants from Zuni settled at Gran Quivira and nearby Pueblo Pardo, joining their inhabitants. These newcomers cremated their dead instead of burying them and made their own style of pottery. Why did they come here? A reasonable speculation is that after Coronado's seizure of Hawikuh (see p. 116) in 1540, some Zunis decided to get out of the path of the conquistadores.

Coronado bypassed Salinas in 1541, and its inhabitants were spared contact with Europeans for two more generations. In 1598, Juan de Oñate, who was establishing a colony to the north of Santa Fe, led 400 mounted troops through Salinas. What an impression they must have made upon the approximately 3,000 Indians at Gran Quivira, most of whom had never seen horses!

The Salinas pueblos made formal submission to the Spanish crown, but the significance of this ritual was probably not understood by the Indians.

Gran Quivira's first church, named after San Isidro, the patron saint of farmers, was built in the 1620s. The church faced east, and in front of it was a small cemetery. Twenty years later, construction began on San Buenaventura Mission. This complex included a much larger church, sacristy, baptistry, dining hall, patio, *convento* (living quarters of the padres), corral, and stables. The church interior is 128 feet long. It is interesting to note, however, that between 1631 and 1659, Gran Quivira did not even have a resident priest, and its religious needs were serviced by the resident priest at Abó, twenty-five miles away. San Buenaventura was excavated and restored between 1923 and 1925 by Edgar Lee Hewett, and in 1951, Gordon Vivian directed excavation of the earlier San Isidro church.

Gran Quivira's distance from the Spanish colonial capital of Santa Fe may have been advantageous in some respects, but its location between two worlds made it vulnerable. In the seventeenth century, relations with the nomadic Apaches deteriorated as the latter grew more predacious. Their frequent raids not only affected Gran Quivira's trading economy but also resulted in loss of life, people taken as slaves, and food stores seized. In 1668, 450 people of the pueblo died of starvation. The sanitary conditions at the mission and pueblo were reportedly abominable, and more Indians died from disease and epidemics. A period of drought, which intensified these conditions, finally made Gran Quivira unlivable. Between 1672 and 1675, the last remnant of the population left the pueblo to join villages along the Rio Grande; their cultural identity was absorbed by the peoples who gave them haven.

Gran Quivira's ruins are worth the time it takes to travel to the site. The extensive excavated remains of the pueblo, which are almost adjacent to the mission ruins, include twenty house complexes, kivas, and plazas that cover approximately seventeen acres. The results of excavations in the pueblo ruins by Alden C. Hayes were published by the National Park Service in *Contributions to Gran Quivira Archaeology* in 1981.

Gran Quivira has a small museum and an interpretive trail through the ruins. There is also a picnic area. Visitors can find restaurants and overnight accommodations in Mountainair.

Suggested reading: *Excavations in a 17th-Century Humano Pueblo, Gran Quivira,* by Gordon Vivian, U. S. National Park Service, Archaeological Research Series 8, Washington, D.C., 1964.

La Purisima Concepción mission at Quarai.

Quarai

Quarai is located in Punta de Agua, 8 miles north of Mountainair on New Mexico 55.

The church at Quarai, or Nuestra Senora de La Purisima Concepción de Cuarac, nestled by a cottonwood grove in a small valley near Punta de Agua, has survived with dignity the erosions and scavengings of time. Its tall and massive stone walls dominate the pastoral environment of the valley. Next to the church and mission ruins are the humble mounds of an Indian pueblo, once called Acolocu, which stood two or three stories high. It predates the mission by several centuries and was inhabited by Indians who spoke the Tiwa language, native to Isleta and Sandia, present-

Franciscan friars founded the mission at Quarai about 1628, and the church and *convento* (living quarters for the padres), the ruins of which we see today, were built in the early 1630s under the supervision of Fray Estevan de Perea. A report from about 1641 states that Quarai had a "very good church, organ and choir, very good provisions for public worship, 658 souls under its administration." But Quarai's story was not so seemingly peaceful.

In 1601, Quarai joined the Indians at Abó in defense against a punitive attack by Spanish forces under Oñate's nephew, Vicente de Zaldivar. After a battle and prolonged seige, Zaldivar reportedly overwhelmed the Indians, killed more than 900, burned Acolocu, and took 200 captives. Although the Spanish report is no doubt greatly exaggerated, the people of Quarai did suffer a devastating defeat.

Under the Franciscans, Quarai was the seat of the Holy Office of the Inquisition in New Mexico. While this designation did not result in executions, investigations were held for such offenses as gossip, heresy, blasphemy, witchcraft, use of love potions, and lack of respect for the clergy by civil authorities. Quarai's last case, in 1668–1670, involved charges of superstition against a German trader named Bernardo Gruber. Gruber was grossly mistreated by his inquisitors and lost his property and ultimately his life in trying to regain his freedom. In the aftermath of the Gruber affair, the Holy Tribunal in Mexico City condemned the conduct of the Quarai officials and withdrew their authority to make arrests.

Geronimo de la Llana, a native of Mexico City and the son of Spanish and Creole parents, was Quarai's best known-priest. A reputedly virtuous man and serious educator, he developed a devoted following during the decade he ran the mission. Fray Geronimo died in 1659, shortly before the quality of life in Salinas went into decline. During the subsequent century, the padre's remains were disinterred and moved three times before finding a final resting place in the crypt of St. Francis Cathedral in Santa Fe. The dozen years after his death witnessed the collapse of the missionary enterprise in Salinas and the disappearance of Spanish influence in the region.

Quarai's history was marked throughout by stress and conflict. Built-in tensions were exacerbated by the demands of the community's *encomendero* on the one hand and the priests on the other. Soldier-settlers felt free to establish themselves in areas under cultivation by the Indians, and they were so powerful that official complaints against them often were ineffective. To oppose them and other civil administrators, the clerics sometimes resorted to using their powers of excommunication. It is difficult to imagine today the effect of this internal strife upon the morale and harmony of the mission; it was certainly not a healthy foundation upon which to confront the problems to come.

In the late 1660s, Salinas was struck by drought, crop failure, famine, and disease. If this was not sufficient, Quarai, along with Tajique, Chilili, Abó, Gran Quivira, and other colonial outposts, were subjected to repeated attacks by Apaches and other Plains nomads. The already weakened settlements soon fell. The Spanish withdrew to strongholds along the northern Rio Grande, and the demoralized Indians found refuge among related native villages also along the river. By 1678, two years before the Pueblo Revolt, Quarai was but a memory.

Quarai has a small museum relating to the Spanish Colonial period, an interpretive trail with signs relating the history of the mission, and an attractive picnic area. Camping facilities can be found at nearby Manzano State Park. Restaurants and motels are available in Mountainair.

Suggested reading: "Quarai: A Turbulent History," by John P. Wilson, in *Salinas: Archaeology, History, Prehistory*, edited by David Grant Noble, School of American Research, Santa Fe, New Mexico, 1982

Abó

Abó is located 1 mile north of U.S. 60, 9 miles west of Mountainair, New Mexico. The entrance from U.S. 60 is signed.

Until the digging of wells, springs and streams were the lifeblood of the desert Southwest. The spring at Abó is a reminder of why this site has been the dwelling place of humans for so many centuries. Water from Abó's spring nourished aboriginal gardens, then quenched the thirst of conquistadores, later fed the boilers of railroad steam engines, and today serves the needs of a small Spanish-American community.

Not many yards north of the spring lie the unexcavated mounds of a large Tompiro pueblo and, adjacent to it, the ruins of San Gregorio de Abó Mission. Like Gran Quivira and Quarai, this church was the product of the formidable missionizing enterprise staged by the Franciscans in seventeenth-century New Mexico. Strategically situated between the salt lagoons and the Rio Grande Valley, and in an area of good piñon nut harvests, Abó was a reasonably wealthy community. It was from the sale of piñon nuts, in fact, that the mission was able to afford the purchase of a church organ in 1661.

The salt beds of Salinas were an important regional commodity.

Traditionally treated as neutral ground, they attracted Indians from far and wide. But the locals had a geographical monopoly and participated actively in the salt trade. A sizable chunk of salt was excavated from a room at Gran Quivira, probably awaiting transport to a distant buyer when the site was abandoned. The Spanish, too, needed salt, though for a different purpose. They had discovered rich deposits of silver in Parral, Mexico, and used large quantities of salt to process the ore. To mine and transport the salt to Parral, they used practices that were forbidden even under their own laws—enforced labor and slavery. But in this remote frontier country, many inconvenient laws written in Spain were unenforceable.

When viewing the ruins of Abó, built by the labor of the local Tompiros, it is startling to think that the mission only functioned for about fifty years. Three hundred of its 350-year existence has been as a ruin. During those two or three generations of use, the Indians at Abó had an uncertain and fluctuating relationship with their Spanish overlords, beginning in 1598 on a note of cordiality, but by 1601, degenerating into open warfare. In this year, the Indians, allied with warriors from Quivira, suffered heavy losses when they were defeated in a six-day fight against Spanish forces. Within a generation, these subjugated Indians were helping to build Abó's mission and tending the gardens of the missionary.

In addition to the main pueblo of Abó, which is next to the church, a second smaller, and perhaps older, ruin lies farther off across the arroyo. It too is unexcavated. The extent of both pueblos can be roughly estimated by traversing the contours of the room blocks and plazas. When Adolph Bandelier visited Abó in the late nineteenth century, he interviewed local residents who remembered seeing, forty years earlier, ruins standing three stories high.

The mission ruins were excavated and restored in the 1930s under the direction of Joseph H. Toulouse, Jr. Toulouse did not find the organ purchased from the sale of nuts but did locate a kiva in the west patio that was built at about the same time as the church. The kiva's existence here is somewhat of a puzzle in view of the priests' common repression of native religious practices. His report also mentions the excavation of turkey pens within the mission walls and the recovery of watermelon and mission grape seeds, both varieties from the Old World. These mission grapes predate the vineyards of southern California by over 100 years. Domestic turkeys, of course, were an important food source of the Anasazi, and the Spanish lost little time in bringing these valuable fowl back across the Atlantic, where they spread rapidly throughout Europe. Their domestication within the mission is but one indication of the two-way exchange

The Abó mission complex.

that occurred when the Pueblo and Spanish cultures met.

At Abó, an interpretive trail leads through the mission and pueblo ruins but the monument has no other facilities. Farther down Abó Canyon, south of the monument, visitors can find many examples of Tompiro rock art. More information about Abó can be learned at the National Park Service's visitor center in Mountainair.

Suggested reading: *The Mission of San Gregorio de Abó,* by Joseph H. Toulouse, Jr., Monograph No. 13, School of American Research, Santa Fe, New Mexico, 1949.

Jemez State Monument

Jemez State Monument is located on New Mexico 4 just north of Jemez Springs, New Mexico. The monument is 55 miles north of Albuquerque and 30 miles southwest of Los Alamos.

The Jemez (hay-mez) Indians live at Walatoa, or Jemez Pueblo, on the southern flank of the Jemez Mountains, west of the Rio Grande Valley. This area has been their homeland for about 700 years. Both oral tradition and archaeological traces suggest that before moving here, the ancestors of the Jemez lived in the upper San Juan River country to the north. Possibly, the Jemez are descended from the Mesa Verde Anasazi.

In 1541, Francisco de Barrio-Nuevo, one of Coronado's captains, penetrated into the southern Jemez Mountains where he counted seven Pueblo villages near Jemez Springs. He named the region the Province of Aguas Calientes after the many hot springs in the area. Fifty-seven years later, Juan de Oñate reported eleven Jemez pueblos. Franciscan missionary work among the Jemez in the early seventeenth century faltered at first. To facilitate the friars' task and simplify administrative control over the Indians, the Spanish authorities consolidated the scattered Jemez communities into three of the existing villages—Patoqua, Astialakwa, and Giusewa. Jemez State Monument protects the ruins of Giusewa.

In 1622, Navajo raids caused the inhabitants to abandon Giusewa and Patoqua and to scatter. The newly built church at Giusewa also was destroyed. Nevertheless, the Franciscan effort persisted, and by 1627, under the leadership of Fray Martin de Avenida, the Jemez people were reassembled and the church, San Jose de los Jemez, was rebuilt.

Throughout its history, this mission was marked by conflict and misfortune. In the mid-1600s, the Jemez made peace with the Navajos and conspired with them to evict the Spaniards. However, the insurgency failed, and in retaliation for the one Spaniard killed, twenty-nine Indians were hung. In 1675, Spanish civil authorities publicly executed on the Santa Fe plaza Pueblo Indians suspected of witchcraft. Among them was one Jemez man. This incident outraged all the Pueblos, and when the Pueblo Revolt broke out five years later, the Jemez joined in. The revolt triumphed, and many of the despised Spanish priests and settlers were killed. The rest were driven out of New Mexico to exile in El Paso. Fray Juan de Jesus Maria at Giusewa Pueblo was among the martyred Franciscans.

Twelve years later, Don Diego de Vargas reconquered the territory and found the Jemez people living in one fortified mesa-top pueblo. From here the Jemez now made war on neighboring Santa Ana and Zia pueblos, which had allied themselves with the Spaniards. Their attacks provoked a punitive strike by Vargas, which drove them from their village and resulted in the deaths of 84 people, with 361 taken prisoner. Vargas also recovered the remains of Fray Maria in whose shoulder an arrow was still embedded. Despite their losses, the valiant Jemez joined the abortive revolt of 1696 and afterwards fled to the Dinetah (see p. 207) in the heart of Navajo country. Some years later, when circumstances permitted, many returned to the Jemez Mountains

San José de los Jemez Church, Jemez State Monument.

and founded Walatoa, where they still live today. It is little wonder that during the seventeenth century the Franciscans considered the Jemez mission to be a hardship post.

In 1921 and 1922, archaeologists from the School of American Research in Santa Fe excavated a section of Giusewa and found that the pueblo predated the church by at least 300 years. The site has never been totally surveyed, but the pueblo mounds are easily recognizable, beginning on the west side of the church and extending across the present highway. It is thought that some portions of the pueblo were three stories in height. Although twenty rooms and two kivas were cleared during the initial excavations, little scientific information was recorded for posterity.

The church and monastery, constructed of sandstone and adobe, with walls varying in thickness from two to eight feet, is considerably more intact than the pueblo. Even in ruins, it is a truly impressive structure, the more so when you consider that no secular architects or engineers were available to assist these early Franciscan priests and their Indian laborers. The interior of the church measures 111 feet in length and is 34 feet wide. Along the sides of the nave stand twelve pedestals that probably supported statues of the disciples.

Perhaps the most exciting discovery in the church ruins was a series of frescoes on the nave walls. The fresco technique, involving the application of paint to wet plaster, was rare in New Mexico ecclesiastical art. Fleur-de-lis and other floral patterns and realistic Indian motifs in green, blue, yellow, red, black, and white were found. Today, they are reproduced in the monument's museum. Also of interest were remnants of windows made of selenite, a translucent form of gypsum. At the rear of the church, an octagonal turret rises forty-two feet above the altar, showing that seventeenth-century New Mexico churches served a defensive as well as religious function. In 1936 and 1937, the adjoining monastery was excavated, including numerous cells used by the Franciscans, a small private chapel, and the remains of a stairway.

Jemez State Monument is administered by the Museum of New Mexico and is open daily except on state holidays. Its small museum has interpretive exhibits relating to New Mexico history and displays of Indian and Spanish artifacts and crafts. The ruins trail passes over the mounds of Giusewa, past an open kiva, through the church and monastery ruins, and into the courtyard. Signs along the path interpret features of historical interest. The monument is nestled at the edge of a narrow valley in piñon- and juniper-covered foothills. This beautiful landscape may compel some visitors to walk or explore farther on their own.

Route 4 to Los Alamos offers an exceptionally scenic drive through the Jemez Mountains, past the Valle Grande (an ancient volcanic crater), to Bandelier National Monument (see p. 175). Camping and picnic areas can be found along the road. A few miles south of the monument is Jemez Pueblo, whose residents are descended from the inhabitants of Giusewa. Jemez's annual Feast Day on 12 November includes plaza dances and a trade fair. This event is open to the public and will be enjoyed by anyone interested in the contemporary life of Pueblo Indians.

Suggested reading: *The Missions of New Mexico, 1776,* by Eleanor B. Adams and Angelico Chavez, University of New Mexico Press, Albuquerque, New Mexico, 1956.

Pueblitos of Dinetah

The Pueblitos of Dinetah are scattered throughout the Largo and Gobernador river drainages northeast of Farmington, New Mexico. To obtain detailed directions to the sites, call the Bureau of Land Management at (505) 761-4504 or (505) 327-5344.

The Dinetah is a large area in northwestern New Mexico that was the original homeland of the Navajos in the Southwest. It also is a place where many Pueblo Indians from the Rio Grande Valley lived as refugees from Spanish rule. Unlike the 800-year-old ruins of the Anasazi in the Four Corners region, the *pueblitos* or small pueblos of Dinetah are of more recent origin—about 1715 to 1754. The Navajo Indians regard the Dinetah as a special, even sacred, place in their history, and the pueblito sites represent an important period in the formation of modern Navajo culture.

The Navajos are an Apachean people who migrated into the northern Southwest sometime prior to the Spanish colonization of the Rio Grande Valley in the late 1500s. Other Apache tribes roamed the plains and mountain regions farther to the east and south. In 1680, both the Navajos and Apaches played a minor supportive role in the Great Pueblo Revolt in which the Pueblo Indians overthrew Spanish rule and drove Spanish colonists and civil authorities out of New Mexico. During subsequent conflicts that arose when Spain reclaimed the northern Rio Grande Valley between 1692 and 1696, many Pueblo Indians abandoned their homes and sought a new place to live where they would be relatively safe from Spanish soldiers. The Navajos were supportive, offering displaced Pueblo people a place of refuge in the Dinetah. Pueblos poured into the region from such villages as San Cristobal, Santa Clara, San Felipe, and Jemez. Later, refugees from Acoma and Awatowi, a Hopi town, also arrived.

The Pueblos and Navajos lived together in the Dinetah for several generations. Eventually, many Pueblo families returned to their Rio Grande homeland, but others chose to remain with the Navajos, sharing their customs and intermarrying with their protectors.

Archaeologists who have studied Dinetah sites believe the pueblitos themselves were not built until after about 1715, when Utes and Comanches began raiding Spanish and Indian settlements in New Mexico. The pueblitos were designed to be highly defensive and clearly were used by a people living in fear of attack. Typically, the fort-like sites are situated on high promontories and on the rims of deep canyons with views in all directions. Many are perched on top of large isolated boulders making access nearly impossible. They were built of uncut sandstone

A pueblito in the Dinetah.

blocks and their style of masonry suggests they were put up in haste. In general appearance, they somewhat resemble the towers of Hovenweep (see p. 51), which were built by ancestral Pueblo Indians centuries before, possibly under similar circumstances.

Near most of the pueblitos are traces of Navajo hogans and roasting pits. The "forked stick" hogans of this period were built by first leaning together three forked poles as a tripod support structure, then placing more poles against these to form a conical framework that was covered by bark and earth. Many of these hogan sites are visible today and a few of the support poles even remain standing.

By 1754, the Navajo and Pueblo people had left the Dinetah. Whether they were forced out by Ute and Spanish attackers or whether they found the region environmentally unsuitable for

The site of a Navajo pictograph stolen from a rock face in the Dinetah region near Bloomfield, New Mexico.

herding sheep and horses is uncertain. But the more than half a century of Navajo and Pueblo coexistence in the Dinetah saw a blending of the two formerly distinct cultural traditions. Some aspects of Pueblo religion and ceremonialism were adopted and modified by the Navajos, and a number of new Navajo clans were formed at this time. The Pueblo use of kivas, on the other hand, was discontinued, and the Navajo language alone came to be spoken.

The time of the Dinetah survived in Navajo story and legend over the generations, but until recent years, not many modern Navajos realized that it was an actual, as well as a mythic, place. Since the 1950s, the Dinetah, which is administered by the Bureau of Land Management, has undergone intensive development by oil and natural gas companies, and today, this once-remote area is covered by a network of dirt roads leading to gas wells. Some roads pass close to the historic pueblitos, resulting in much damage from this uncontrolled exposure.

Recently, the Bureau of Land Management has stabilized eight pueblitos and opened them up to public visitation as part of its national "Adventures in the Past" program. Persons interested in visiting the pueblitos, however, should be forewarned about several difficulties. First, to get to the sites you may have to drive forty to a hundred miles on dirt roads that can be dusty or muddy depending on the weather. After heavy rains, some roads become impassable because of gullies, washouts, and mud. A four-wheel-drive vehicle or pick-up truck is recommended for travel in this area. Second, even with the help of a map, it is easy to lose your way in the maze of unmarked roads. Finally, to negotiate some of the trails to the sites demands surefootedness and physical fitness.

While explorations in the Dinetah are not for everyone, the pueblitos are rewarding for the unique insight they give into early Navajo and Pueblo history. Travel services can be found in Bloomfield and Farmington. Other nearby archaeological sites include Salmon Ruins (see p. 131), Aztec Ruins National Monument (see p. 127), and Chaco Canyon (see p. 119).

Suggested reading: "Navajo Prehistory and History to 1850," by David M. Brugge, in *Handbook of North American Indians*, vol. 10, edited by Alfonso Ortiz, Smithsonian Institution, Washington, D.C., 1983.

AFTERWORD
The Future of the Past in the Southwest

Native Americans have been living in the Southwest for at least 10,000 years, leaving behind them thousands of traces of their existence. These archaeological sites range from barely discernible scatters of stone flakes to multistoried pueblos and elaborate pictograph panels. Whatever their character, most of these sites have remained relatively undisturbed for a long time.

As we move into the 1990s, the future of the Southwest's archaeological heritage appears increasingly uncertain. Surrounding and underlying ancient campsites, pithouses, pueblos, and petroglyphs are vast, untapped natural resources, including oil, gas, uranium, coal, and various minerals. The processes involved in extracting this wealth often stand in direct opposition to preserving the region's fragile environment, including its cultural heritage.

Preceding energy and mineral development has been population growth. Villages and cities are expanding, roads multiplying and widening, utility lines crisscrossing wide desert expanses, and sightseers and hikers penetrating traditionally remote areas. The result of increasing population and mobility has been, and no doubt will continue to be, increased wear and tear, if not outright destruction, of archaeological remains.

A third phenomenon, pothunting, has long been a problem to archaeological preservation. When old Indian pots command high prices in an international market, the temptation to dig, buy, sell, and collect has become even more irresistible. Probe sticks and shovels have often become supplanted by bulldozers, which can churn over an entire prehistoric village site in a matter of hours. In recent years, unscrupulous entrepreneurs have reaped profits at the expense of these ancient ruins. The looting of America's ancient heritage, although most dramatically witnessed in the Southwest, is a serious national problem.

Archaeological preservation lies in the shadow of many more pressing and publicized national and regional issues. The Archaeological Resources Protection Act of 1979, some excerpts of which are cited on the following pages, was a significant step forward. What is most needed now is public education, law enforcement, and legislation to curtail the export of American antiquities. What can you do to help preserve our country's archaeological heritage? Let legislators know how you feel, especially when specific land-use issues are being debated. Join state and regional groups such as the Arizona Site Steward Program (Arizona Historic Preservation Office, 800 West Washington Street, Phoenix, Arizona 85007), whose volunteers adopt and monitor sites, learn about them, and report problems. The Bureau of Land Management and U. S. Forest Service have similar programs. Support the Archaeological Conservancy (415 Orchard Drive, Santa Fe, New Mexico 87501), a national, nonprofit, membership organization dedicated to preserving archaeological sites.

The greatest help in preserving archaeological ruins will come from the vast pool of people who love the Southwest's cultural and natural environments. These include hunters, fishermen, hikers, backpackers, bird watchers, horseback riders, photographers, naturalists, ruins buffs, and many others. Not long ago, the photographer/pilot, Paul Logsdon, was flying his plane over the Galisteo Basin in New Mexico. When he spotted a couple of human legs dangling out of a hole in the Pueblo Shay ruins, he radioed the state police, and shortly thereafter, a pothunter was caught.

America's archaeological sites are a national treasure, valuable to all people, of all ethnic backgrounds, for all time. They are an inspiration to writers and artists and an irreplaceable source of information to historians, social scientists, tourists, and school children. They are sacred to Native Americans. In the light of their worth, reasonable compromises must be made by government officials and energy developers to ensure that generations to come will know about our past.

I hope this book will help generate wider public appreciation of southwestern antiquity and will have a positive influence on preserving this heritage for the future.

Archaeological Resources Protection Act of 1979

PUBLIC LAW 96-95, 31 OCTOBER 1979

To protect archaeological resources on public lands and Indian lands, and for other purposes.

FINDINGS AND PURPOSE

Sec. 2(a) The Congress finds that—

(1) archaeological resources on public lands and Indian lands are an accessible and irreplaceable part of the Nation's heritage;

(2) these resources are increasingly endangered because of their commercial attractiveness;

(3) existing Federal laws do not provide adequate protection to prevent the loss and destruction of these archaeological resources and sites resulting from uncontrolled excavations and pillage; and

(4) there is a wealth of archaeological information which has been legally obtained by private individuals for noncommercial purposes and which could voluntarily be made available to professional archaeologists and institutions.

(b) The purpose of this Act is to secure, for the present and future benefit of the American people, the protection of archaeological resources and sites which are on public lands and Indian lands, and to foster increased cooperation and exchange of information between governmental authorities, the professional archaeological community, and private individuals having collections of archaeological resources and data which were obtained before the date of the enactment of this Act.

PROHIBITED ACTS AND CRIMINAL PENALTIES

Sec. 6(a) No person may excavate, remove, damage, or otherwise alter or deface any archaeological resource located on public lands or Indian lands unless such activity is pursuant to a permit issued under section 4, a permit referred to in section 4(h)(2), or the exemption contained in section 4(g)(l).

(b) No person may sell, purchase, exchange, transport, receive, or offer to sell, purchase, or exchange any archaeological resource if such resource was excavated or removed from public lands or Indian lands in violation of—

(1) the prohibition contained in subsection (a), or

(2) any provision, rule, regulation, ordinance, or permit in effect under any other provision of Federal law.

(c) No person may sell, purchase, exchange, transport, receive, or offer to sell, purchase, or exchange, in interstate or foreign commerce, any archaeological resource excavated, removed, sold, purchased, exchanged, transported, or received in violation of any provision, rule, regulation, ordinance, or permit in effect under State or local law.

(d) Any person who knowingly violates, or counsels, procures, solicits, or employs any other person to violate, any prohibition contained in subsection (a), (b), or (c) of this section shall, upon conviction, be fined not more than $10,000 or imprisoned not more than one year, or both; *Provided, however,* That if the commercial or archaeological value of the archaeological resources involved and the cost of restoration and repair of such resources exceeds the sum of $5,000, such person shall be fined not more than $20,000 or imprisoned not more than two years, or both. In the case of a second or subsequent such violation upon conviction such person shall be fined not more than $100,000, or imprisoned not more than five years, or both.

REWARDS; FORFEITURE

Sec. 8. (a) Upon the certification of the Federal land manager concerned, the Secretary of the Treasury is directed to pay from penalties and fines collected under sections 6 and 7 an amount equal to one-half of such penalty or fine, but not to exceed $500, to any person who furnishes information which leads to the finding of a civil violation, or the conviction of criminal violation, with respect to which such penalty or fine was paid. If several persons provided such information, such amount shall be divided among such persons. No officer or employee of the United States or of any State or local government who furnishes information or renders service in the performance of his official duties shall be eligible for payment under this subsection.

Index